KEYS TO UNDERSTANDING AND TEACHING YOUR BIBLE

THOMAS E. FOUNTAIN

THOMAS NELSON PUBLISHERS
Nashville • Camden • New York

Library of Congress Cataloging in Publication Data
Fountain, Thomas E.
  Keys to understanding and teaching your Bible.

  Bibliography: p. 223
  Includes index.
    1. Bible—Hermeneutics.   2. Bible—Language, style.
  I. Title.
  BS476.F68   1983   220.6'01   83-2224
  ISBN 0-8407-5826-X

CONTENTS

Preface 7

PART I: *General Keys to Understanding Scripture*

1. Biblical Interpretation: Some Basics 11
2. The Right Attitude 21
3. The Right Method 26
4. Accurate Reading 37
5. The Meaning of Individual Words 42
6. The Context 51
7. Parallel Passages 59
8. The Historical Background 67
9. The Purpose, Plan, and Limitations of Each Book
   74
10. The Key to Both Testaments 81

PART II: *Special Keys to Understanding Scripture*

11. Figures of Speech 91
12. Hebrew Idioms 105
13. Types 118
14. Symbols 125
15. Parables 132
16. Allegories 153
17. Fables, Riddles, Enigmas, and Proverbs 156
18. Hebrew Poetry 163

19. The Interpretation of Prophecy 173
20. Scriptural Quotations 188
21. Historical Contradictions 198
22. Doctrinal Difficulties 206
    Suggested Books for Bible Students 216
    Bibliography 223
    Index of Texts Mentioned 226

PREFACE

Over the years 1953 to 1956, while serving as a missionary in Mexico City, I taught a course in biblical interpretation in a small Spanish-speaking Bible school. To provide my students with a suitable textbook, I published *Claves de Interpretación Bíblica (Keys to Biblical Interpretation)*. The book has since gone to seven printings, and currently an eighth is being prepared.

For years I resisted my wife's suggestion that I prepare a similar book in English. But recently, after further experience teaching a class of young adults, I became convinced that such a book would be helpful to English-speaking teachers and students in our own country. It is primarily for them that this volume has been prepared.

I must acknowledge my indebtedness to Dr. Robert C. McQuilkin, founder and president of Columbia (S.C.) Bible College and my highly esteemed teacher in this field. His death in 1952 prevented him from fulfilling his plan to write a text on the subject. This book is basically an expansion of notes taken in his classes and to that extent reflects his own teaching.

It is my hope and prayer that the study of the neglected subject of biblical interpretation may quicken interest in Bible reading and ease what is often a difficult assignment for teachers: that of teaching the most important book in the world.

Biblical quotations used here are normally taken from the New King James Version (NKJV). But occasional reference is made to the King James Version (KJV), the American Standard Version (ASV), the New American Standard Bible (NASB), the Revised Standard Version (RSV), the New International Version (NIV), the New English Bible (NEB), the Good News Bible (GNB), the Living Bible, and the Phillips translation of the New Testament.

Part I
GENERAL KEYS TO UNDERSTANDING SCRIPTURE

1
BIBLICAL INTERPRETATION: SOME BASICS

For every student and teacher of the Bible, two questions are of primary importance: What does the Bible *say* on any given matter, and what does the Bible *mean* by what it says?

The answer to the first question may be supplied by diligent reading of the biblical text, or careful consultation with the proper reference books, or both. In all modern versions of the Bible, the attempt has been made to make the text clear and accessible to the reader with average scholastic achievements.

Even so, the meaning of a passage often escapes the reader for one or more good reasons. Consequently, the answer to the second question becomes the more important one. The study of biblical interpretation deals with this question of meaning.

The practice of interpreting the Bible text is first described in the Book of Deuteronomy. Beginning in chapter 4 of that book, Moses repeated the laws given earlier at Sinai. But as he did so, he expanded the meaning and application of many laws, presumably to make them clearer, less open to misunderstanding. That restatement of the law is to be construed as biblical interpretation, perhaps the earliest recorded effort in this direction.

Centuries later, following the return from the Babylonian Exile, Ezra the scribe and others read the Hebrew text in the presence of all the people. They "read distinctly from the book...[*with an interpretation*, says the ASV marginal note] and they gave the sense, and helped them to understand the reading" (Neh. 8:1–8).

The present-day discipline of interpretation, as taught in many seminaries and Bible institutes, has been known as a scientific pursuit only in recent centuries. Its earliest beginnings were with the Jewish teacher Hillel, who lived from 30 B.C. to A.D. 9. He formulated seven rules for biblical interpretation.[1] But only since the time of Martin Luther has the science of biblical interpretation grown to be a significant part of the usual biblical and theological studies.

Biblical interpretation is known as *hermeneutics*, a word derived from the Greek verb *hermeneuō*, to interpret. As a discipline, it includes whatever rules may be necessary to explain the meaning of any literary passage, especially the text of the Bible. Rules that help us understand and explain the Bible, derived from any source, constitute the subject of hermeneutics.

If in practice we were to apply this description in its broadest sense to the study of hermeneutics, we would include many things that do not properly belong to it. At the same time, this definition of hermeneutics recognizes the contribution of those many subjects and seeks to include them as necessary background for the interpreter.

A pamphlet issued by the Vernon C. Grounds

---

[1]Eduard Lohse, *The New Testament Environment* (Nashville: Abingdon, 1976), p. 171.

Learning Center at Denver (1980) informs us that:

To skillfully interpret and communicate the Book, a scholar must interact with other books—books about Hebrew, Greek, archeology, missions, history, theology, education, counseling, science, homiletics, literature, music—all contribute to an understanding of the Bible and the people who need its message.

On the value of knowing the original languages, A. Berkeley Mickelsen says: "If the student does not know Greek, Hebrew, or Aramaic, then he should check a good commentary (on matters which may affect meaning)."[2]

When the Bible student does not have access to such a commentary, the best alternative will be to read the text in various translations in order to determine the sense of the text. Ruth Graham, wife of the well-known evangelist, keeps at hand for study more than twenty versions in order to better understand the ideas that the Holy Spirit had in mind when He inspired that text.[3]

The Bible interpreter should make an effort to learn everything possible of these widely varying subjects. Most of all, hermeneutics emphasizes the rules of interpretation that derive from the study of the *characteristics of human language*, whether they appear in sacred or secular literature.

The Languages of Hermeneutics

Every language has its own typical expressions that

---

[2]A. Berkeley Mickelsen, *Interpreting the Bible* (Grand Rapids: Eerdmans, 1963), p. 16.

[3]Billy Graham, *The Holy Spirit* (New York: Warner Books, 1980), p. 62.

do not lend themselves to literal translation into other languages. Idioms, proverbs, grammatical peculiarities, or references to local customs or circumstances may present problems for the interpreter whose language is different from that of the original writer. Even for speakers of the same language, some usages may be hard to understand.

Interpreting the languages of the Bible involves a special set of problems. The Bible was written in another age, separated from the present by nearly two millenia. The part of the world where its events took place is removed from us by an ocean and a continent. Two of the languages in which it was written are—or were for many years—dead languages. They do not even belong to the Germanic family of languages to which English belongs. Hebrew, Aramaic, and Greek have only the remotest connection with English.

When we attempt to study Hebrew, we find that it uses a strange alphabet, writes from right to left instead of left to right, and originally had only one or two vowels. In later years vowel markings were added, composed of dots and dashes and a few other marks. For the most part, we have no literature in Hebrew other than the Old Testament. The Hebrews left almost no other written materials: the apocryphal writings, the "Dead Sea Scrolls," and some broken pieces of pottery are about all we have.[4] Our studies must be based on the biblical text. Even modern Israelis have to approach the study of Hebrew the same

---

[4]While the Dead Sea Scrolls are best known for their biblical texts, a rather large number of extra-biblical writings have been found among them, such as biblical commentaries, the rules of conduct governing several religious communities, psalms, and hymns, and certain apocryphal writings.

way, because biblical Hebrew has not been spoken for hundreds of years.

The case of New Testament Greek is very different. Greek has been continuously spoken at least since the fourth century before Christ. The Greek of the New Testament can be understood today with some study by any well-educated speaker of modern Greek. And although the Hebrews left only a very few copies of their Scriptures, there are hundreds of manuscripts in the popular Greek of the New Testament era. Most of the manuscripts that survived were written on parchment or vellum, although some fragments remain of manuscripts written on fragile papyrus. Early in the eighteenth century important discoveries were made in Egypt of Greek materials written on papyrus and preserved accidentally in the extremely dry atmosphere of that country. These papyri have thrown a great deal of light on the characteristics of the popular Greek of that period, known as *koinē* (common) Greek.

However, the Egyptian papyri do not include New Testament documents. In general, the papyri are classified in two categories: literary works and documents, both official and private. Studies based on the *koinē* have added greatly to our understanding of the New Testament.

For those reasons, studying New Testament Greek is much easier than studying Hebrew and, fortunately, of greater value to the average student of the Scriptures. Nevertheless, access to information about both languages is essential for the interpreter. And lest we ignore the Aramaic portions of Scripture, it should be noted that Aramaic is normally studied as part of the Hebrew language, because it was a dialect in widespread use from the earliest history of the Hebrews.

The Free Examination of the Scripture

If we conclude that the study of hermeneutics is necessary to a proper understanding of the Bible, it may seem contradictory to say that there is a universal ability to grasp its message. It is clear that God intended for all people to give due attention to that message, even before they believe it. Evangelicals affirm that all people not only have the right to read and understand the Bible for themselves, but they have the obligation before God to read and understand it as best they can. That is to say, every individual who has access to a copy of the Bible and who knows how to read is obligated to do so.

This truth does not eliminate the need for teachers within the church. Nor do we pretend that every lay person ought to be completely instructed by the Bible alone, independently of other believers. In the first place, it is doubtful that any Christian could receive the necessary instruction without the help of others. In the second place, no human instruction is ever complete or perfect; no teacher other than Jesus Himself ever taught perfectly. And in the third place, the Holy Spirit chooses certain individuals to be teachers of the Word of God and helps them carry out their function by appropriate gifts of the Spirit.

But the most obvious reason every person ought to read and understand the Bible is the Bible's clear teaching on this subject:

These were more fair-minded...in that they received the word with all readiness, and searched the Scriptures daily to find out whether these things were so (Acts 17:11).

I charge you by the Lord that this epistle be read to all the holy brethren (1 Thess. 5:27).

From childhood you have known the Holy Scriptures. . . . All Scripture is given by inspiration of God, and is profitable for doctrine, for reproof, for correction, for instruction in righteousness, that the man of God may be complete, thoroughly equipped for every good work (2 Tim. 3:15-17).

The principle of open access to the Bible expressed in these texts was proclaimed at the beginning of the Reformation under the name "Free Examination (of the Scriptures)." Every evangelical confession affirms or takes for granted this principle.

Opponents of "Free Examination" often twist the meaning of the phrase. They say the principle consists of the right to interpret freely and privately according to "the ideas, passions and prejudices" of the reader, or according to "individual inspiration."[5]

But the principle is called "Free Examination" not "Free Interpretation." The liberty it declares exists for every individual because it is given by God, and because no one has dominion over another's faith (2 Cor. 1:24). The liberty we enjoy is with regard to other people. With respect to God, every reader has the personal obligation to examine the Bible for himself, but he does *not* have the freedom to interpret it according to his own pleasure. Peter declared this plainly: "knowing this first, that no prophecy of Scripture is of any private interpretation, for prophecy never came by the will of man, but holy men of God spoke as they were moved by the Holy Spirit" (2

---

[5]From the General Introduction to the Torres Amat Version of the Bible, *La Sagrada Biblia*, 1st ed. (Santiago, Chile: *Revista Católica*, 1946).

Pet. 1:20–21). God's Word has the meaning He gave to it, and we must attempt to understand that meaning.

The Application of the Rules

At the outset we should point out that not every rule of interpretation will be applicable in every case. The various rules are to be applied by the interpreter only when they may resolve a particular problem. Clearly, the skill of the interpreter will influence the interpretation one gives to the text, especially in the care with which one's knowledge is applied.

Adequate interpretation is within the grasp of anyone who skillfully applies the rules of hermeneutics. On this matter Mickelsen writes:

Balance (in interpreting the Bible) involves not only an awareness of the elements but *also a coordination of the elements*. If I want to swim the various strokes correctly, I can sit down with a swimming manual and find out exactly what the arms and legs are supposed to do. But when I get into the water and try to coordinate all of my muscles so that I glide easily through the water, I find that coordination is a skill to be mastered, not a series of rules to be memorized. So it is in interpretation. It takes skill to bring together all the elements needed to interpret any one passage correctly.[6]

Not every text will require special interpretation, since the great majority will be perfectly understandable to people of normal intelligence. Some texts will require interpretation only for those whose educational background is insufficient to allow them to grasp

---

[6]Mickelsen, *Interpreting the Bible*, pp. 375–376.

the sense of the passage. For such persons the interpreter may find it necessary to explain facts that others already know or merely to simplify the language. Other texts will be difficult for the great majority of readers, and some will remain a mystery even to the most skilled interpreters.

As suggested by the title of this book, the principles of hermeneutics may be regarded as *keys* to many kinds of biblical problems. They may also be compared to a box of tools. When a master carpenter sets out to build a house, construct a piece of furniture, or do some repair work, he first considers the problems presented by the project. He then selects the tools that will best help do the job. This is exactly what we as interpreters do. We consider the problem or problems presented by the text and then choose the rules that seem to hold the greatest possibilities for resolving the difficulties. In some cases we may have to try a number of rules or use several rules, just as the carpenter uses not only a hammer and saw, but a plane, a chisel, and sandpaper.

The Two Divisions of Hermeneutics

The study of biblical interpretation is usually divided into two parts: general hermeneutics and special hermeneutics. General hermeneutics includes all those rules that may be applied to the Bible as literature. Special hermeneutics includes the rules and considerations needed to interpret special categories of literature, which may contain figurative language, poetry, or prophecy and a variety of special problems. This study will follow that plan.

For Review

1. Define the term "hermeneutics."
2. What is meant by the phrase "Free Examination"?
3. Give some reasons why the Bible presents problems of interpretation.

2
THE RIGHT ATTITUDE

Any legitimate interpreta-tion of the Scriptures calls for spiritual preparation on the part of the interpreter. Readers of the Bible who do not have the right attitude toward the Scriptures, toward the church, toward God and His Son Jesus Christ, and toward His expressions of love and concern for a lost world will soon fall into error. A right attitude is a basic requirement for every serious interpreter of Scripture.

But this attitude is necessarily preceded by the presence of God's Holy Spirit in the one who would interpret His Word. Without Him, the individual is not to be considered a Christian, according to Paul's teaching in Romans 8:9. Those who would attempt to teach others without having the Spirit of God will be "blind leaders of the blind" (Matt. 15:14; 2 Pet. 1:9). It was in order that the followers of Christ might understand the things of God that His Spirit was given to His people (see 1 Cor. 2:12). Evangelicals believe that every true believer is in fact a possessor of the Holy Spirit and is indwelt by Him.

As a fruit of this initial gift of God's Spirit, the interpreter will manifest humility and an openness to learning. Since the Bible is assumed to be the Word of

God, the reader will have the proper respect for its Author and will listen to His voice as a creature before the Creator, a servant before the Master, and a subject in the presence of the King.

The interpreter should also exhibit humility before other believers, since they too may have minds gifted by the same Spirit. Often other readers of the Bible have greater understanding of a particular text, and humility alone will allow the interpreter to accept the truth that God has revealed to another. The interpreter should never think of himself as infallible, even when he is sure in his own mind that he has discovered some truth revealed to him by the Lord.

The apostle Paul has given us a beautiful example of this spirit in Galatians 1:11–12. Paul had received his gospel directly from God the Son. Nevertheless, he went to Jerusalem, impelled to do so by the Spirit Himself, to lay before the other apostles the message he preached. This he did, "lest by any means I might run, or had run, in vain" (Gal. 2:2). The attitude of humility, even before others, is a basic requirement for the interpreter of Scripture.

Reverence before the divine revelation is likewise required of the interpreter. Often we want to subject certain teachings to our own judgment, or look for a way to dismiss them, appealing to an "intellectual" view of the world. As often as not, intellectualism is nothing more than unbelief disguised with respectability.

Sometimes the doctrines of other denominations are held up to ridicule in an irreverent spirit. The way some churches baptize is often the subject of jokes, or their view of the Lord's Supper, of predestination, of sin, or of the democratic conduct of business meetings. Even when the interpreter cannot agree on such doctrines, a spirit of reverence is the only appropriate one for the Bible interpreter. It is even possible that God might withhold His illumination from us so long as we lack reverence in the face of the teachings of other Christians.

In certain rare cases, the language of Scripture may give rise to irreverent thoughts. This would be particularly true of passages such as 2 Kings 18:27 or Ezekiel 23:3. The mere reading of the sinful acts committed by people mentioned in the Bible may set off a train of thought contrary to the purpose for which it was written. In all such cases the Bible reader must strive to read, think, and teach with all due reverence.

Beyond the presence of the Holy Spirit, humility, and reverence, the student of Scripture should strive to keep a spirit of obedience to God. Without it, the interpreter will not be able to communicate God's message rightly to any hearers. One result may be that the reader will not present the truth of Scripture with the appropriate force of conviction, or he may alter the message in line with his own disobedience to it.

In John 5:39–40, we find such a case: Jesus referred to the custom of the Jews to "search the Scriptures" without coming to believe in the one of whom they testified. Since they refused to recognize that Jesus was indeed the promised Messiah, they would not come to Him in faith, nor would they teach the obvious Scriptural truth about Him.

In short, the spirit of obedience requires that the reader be ready and willing to put into practice the things learned in studying the Bible.

Romans 15:4 tells us that "whatever things were written before were written for our learning, that we through the patience and comfort of the Scriptures might have hope." Reference is made here to the personal application of biblical teaching to our personal lives. We are to let its message sink into our hearts and minds so that we may come into line with its ultimate purpose. The basic truths contained in the Bible, its history, the examples set forth in those who either obeyed or disobeyed God, its instructions for living, are to be embraced with complete sincerity and with the purpose of following the Lord.

When we read that God worked mightily on behalf of His ancient people, and through the miracles of Jesus, we are to understand that He is able to do similar things for us today; not necessarily in the same manner, but showing the same love and power toward us in ways appropriate to our times. This is usually accomplished in response to our prayer and faith; so these attitudes should be part of the spirit in which we handle the Scriptures.

Unfortunately, in many cases, the need for devotional use of the Bible is substituted for its deep study; this ought not to be done. Nor should the eager search for the Bible's exact meaning take the place of devotional study; both activities are needed in their own right. Together with the academic pursuit of meaning, one must also sit at Jesus' feet like Mary and learn from Him (Luke 10:39), mixing the word with faith, for genuine profit (Heb. 4:2).

For Review

1. What are the various elements of the proper spirit in which to read and teach the Scriptures? There are at least five.

2. Can you think of other appropriate attitudes that
   ought to characterize the interpreter of Scripture?
   Examine carefully 2 Timothy 2:15, and all of 1
   Thessalonians 2.

3
THE RIGHT METHOD

Proper interpretation depends on a variety of elements. Even with sincerity, humility, reverence, and prayer, Bible interpreters will not be able to arrive at proper conclusions without using the right method. Erroneous ideas concerning the intentions of the writer of the book, the validity of the doctrinal statements, the historical accuracy of the content, and the divine origin of the text will lead the interpreter to false or incomplete conclusions.

To claim that there is a correct method is by no means pretentious. The right method has been determined by a process of elimination; the false methods were eliminated as a result of seeing the false conclusions they produced.

There are three mistaken methods of interpretation in common use, and they will be examined here. Each one has something in its favor. But when any of these approaches is rigidly applied, the error in it is made evident.

The Rationalistic Method

This method consists of subjecting all Scripture to

human reason to determine the validity or historicity of its statements. It presupposes that the supernatural does not exist, and that every text may be understood through the use of human reason. It claims to be the scientific method since it rejects any appeal to the supernatural, according to the scientific approach that prevails in laboratories and most educational centers.

But in so doing, it violates the basic tenet of the scientific method that requires the scientist to begin with an open mind; he is not to judge what he investigates before he has gathered all the data on the subject. Those who use the rationalistic method begin by rejecting one of the fundamental claims of the Bible: that God intervenes in a supernatural way in the affairs of human beings. The rationalists proceed to interpret the Scriptures using their anti-supernatural prejudice as a basis. As a result, they draw conclusions satisfactory to themselves but which are very different from what the Scriptures clearly teach.

This rejection of the supernatural was particularly in vogue during the nineteenth century and continues to prevail in some circles today. Nevertheless, we must note that it has lost much ground in recent times, even among the most liberal theologians.

The rationalistic interpreter considers that supernatural events of the Bible were nothing more than natural occurrences, capable of being explained by physical laws that we now understand, or perhaps by facts that the writers did not know or mention. The rationalist approach holds that the Gospel writers did not intend to deceive their readers but wrote in the conviction that they were telling the truth. For example, the rationalist solves the case of the feeding of the five thousand (see Matt. 14:15-21) by supposing that the generosity of the young boy stimulated others in the crowd to share their food also. No supernatural work is seen in the event. However, the rationalist adds that there was a *moral* miracle in the spontaneous generosity of the people.

In the account of Jesus' walking on the water of the Sea of Galilee, (see Matt. 14:22–33) the rationalists offer a clever solution. They suggest that since the disciples had rowed for many hours during the night and through the storm, they did not realize that they were now close to the shore. Jesus came to be with them, not walking on the water but along the shore. At night, this appearance of the Lord seemed miraculous to them. These interpreters refer to the preposition "on," which in the original Greek (*epi*) may be translated "along side of." In their reading of the text Jesus was not walking *on* the water, but *along side of* it, on the shore. Furthermore they point out that immediately after Jesus entered the boat, the disciples found themselves at their destination.

Following the same method, they find rational explanations for all the supernatural events of the Bible. When this is not possible, they find it necessary to say that the text is not correct or that the writers were mistaken. We should note that these interpreters grasp at any detail that may be construed in their favor, but they reject whatever might show the falseness of their conclusions.

Over the years there have been a number of modifications in the rationalistic method, some of which may help us to understand better the story of the gospel and the Gospel texts. About the middle of the nineteenth century J.C.K. von Hofman of Erlangen developed the idea of "salvation history" (*Heilsgeschichte*)[1] in the Scriptures. For him the most important thing was not the biblical text but the story itself. According to this method, the interpreter is permitted to analyze the text as long as he does so in light of the overall theme of the story. Even though this method contributes something to the study of sacred history, the interpreter may take liberties with the text that are contrary to the general conviction of conservative interpreters.

In 1919 Martin Dibelius published his work "The History of Forms in the Gospels" (*Die Formesgeschichte des Evangeliums*).[2] This type of literary criticism attempted to determine the traditional oral form of the gospel behind the written form in the Gospels. Those who follow this method classify the stories as authoritative declarations, miracles, stories of Jesus, and various sayings. The latter category is divided into sayings of wisdom, prophetic and apocalyptic sayings, laws and regulations for the community, sayings that begin with the word "I", and parables.

This kind of analysis concentrates on the literary form rather than on the truth of the original history. Sometimes the stories are called "myths" or "legends." Nevertheless, this method is helpful in the study of the Gospels as it seeks to explain seeming contradictions between parallel Gospel accounts.

Rudolph Bultmann went far beyond others in his study of the compilation of the Gospels. In 1921 he

---

[1]Bernard Ramm, *Handbook of Contemporary Theology* (Grand Rapids: Eerdmans, 1966), p. 55.

[2]Everett F. Harrison, ed., *Baker's Dictionary of Theology* (Grand Rapids: Eerdmans, 1950), p. 227.

published his work, *The History of the Synoptic Tradition (Die Geschichte der Synoptischen Tradition)*. Among other things, Bultmann says that the act of God in Christ is the foundation of the church and of its preaching (*kērugma*). According to him, the Gospel history is largely composed of myths that imitate the forms of Jewish and Greek myths. The work of the interpreter is to locate these myths and glean the original preaching (*kērugma*) of the church from them.[3] He calls this process "demythologizing"; that is, taking myths out of the New Testament in order to discover the original gospel proclamation.

These methods must be considered variations of the rationalistic method. There is value in the method that examines the history of salvation (*heilsgeschichte*) and that which studies its literary forms (*formesgeschichte*). But in Bultmann's demythologizing, there is too much opportunity for distortion of the Scriptures.

We should not dismiss the rationalistic method without affirming that human intelligence is a gift of God and must be employed responsibly. Our intelligence was not given to be a source of stumbling; it is to be used in the proper study of the divine revelation, being illuminated by the Holy Spirit. Faith and reason are not opposed to one another, especially when one's reason is the product of a healthy mind obedient to God's revelation.

The Allegorical Method

This common approach to the Bible assumes that the Bible was written as a series of allegories. It holds also that it is not the natural, evident meaning that

---

[3]Ramm, *Handbook of Contemporary Theology*, pp. 33–34.

gives the Bible its importance but the "mystical" sense, which means its hidden or spiritual sense.

This method originated with the Hellenistic scholars who sought to resolve the tension between the myths of the gods and the increasing knowledge of science and philosophy. Christian believers in Alexandria, who were incapable of explaining certain kinds of difficulties in the Scriptures, adopted this method in order to commend the Scriptures and the Christian faith to some of the cultured unbelievers. Even though the method was opposed by the Christian leadership in Antioch, Paul's letters contain several allegorical interpretations of Old Testament texts. This approach has influenced the whole history of interpretation from early centuries to the present. It flourished especially during the Middle Ages. Today, the Roman Catholic church holds certain doctrines that sprang from this method. Evangelical Protestants base certain beliefs on the allegorical method: for example, amillennialists interpret much of the Book of Revelation as allegories describing the church.

One example of the way the allegorical method is abused may be seen in the treatment given to Daniel's experience in the lion's den (Dan. 6). Some interpreters would say Daniel was not in a literal lion's den but was merely imprisoned by the temptations and weaknesses common to men. These spiritual problems are represented by the lions. Daniel's faith preserved him from harm, while his enemies fell victim to those same temptations. The lesson contained in the story is that only the one who has faith in God can overcome all the difficulties in life.

There is a sense in which certain events of the Bible may be allegorized or spiritualized. Historical events may provide examples or illustrations of a spiritual truth *but only when the historical and literal sense of the story is first acknowledged.* Otherwise, the result is a false interpretation of the biblical text. Preachers often present allegories in sermons that are otherwise biblically sound.

Another example of abusing the allegorical method is the story of our first parents in the Garden of Eden (Gen. 2–3). An interpreter may understand the tree of the knowledge of good and evil, not literally, but as a reference to sexual intercourse. From this we have the popular use of the forbidden fruit (see Gen. 2:17) as a symbol of sexual activity, even though the biblical account makes no such suggestion.

There are, however, some allegories in the Bible, often hard to identify because they are not usually referred to as allegories. A rare exception is Galatians 4:24–31, where Paul gives the story of Abraham, Sarah, and Hagar an allegorical interpretation. But its historical character is not placed in any doubt; the Holy Spirit has added an allegorical sense to the story in order to point out the difference between the two Testaments. Other allegories will be identified in Chapter 16, where they are treated as a special type of figurative language.

Frequently interpreters who abuse the allegorical method will set aside important facts of the biblical history and text and cause serious damage to the clear sense of Scripture. The principles of this method are so ambiguous that it easily lends itself to this sort of abuse.

The Dogmatic Method

This is the third faulty method of interpretation. Its

name comes from the Greek word *dogma*, which means "teaching." Properly speaking, all Christian doctrines are dogmas, even though, unfortunately, the word has a certain negative connotation for the popular mind. This is due to the fact that Christian doctrines have often been taught in a rigid or hostile spirit. However, a more valid reason for objecting to the dogmatic method is because *it interprets according to the dogmas of a particular group*. The interpretation of Scripture is considered authoritative because it proceeds from the religious authority and tradition of a group, and not because it is based on accepted principles of interpretation. If one believes that the church or a particular group within the church has been charged with the responsibility of interpreting the Scriptures for the rest of the world, the dogmatic method is reasonable enough.

Among the Jews it is common to apply Isaiah 53, not to the sufferings of the Messiah but to the nation of Israel as a whole, primarily because this has become the traditional interpretation given to it by their rabbis.

A number of Catholic doctrines illustrate the dogmatic method. One of the best known is the doctrine based on Matthew 16:18–19, the passage describing the apostle Simon as Peter "the rock." From this text Roman Catholic theologians draw the teaching that Peter was the first pope and the foundation of the church. The passage presents difficulties for anyone who would give it an unbiased and adequate interpretation. But an impartial examination of it yields no basis for teaching that Jesus would build His church upon the person of Peter, the first in a long line of apostolic succession. Nevertheless, the doctrine of papal infallibility is based on this view, and adherents of the Roman Catholic faith interpret the passage according to the dogmatic method.

Not only do the Roman Catholics often employ this method; the large majority of evangelical Christians usually interpret certain passages of the Bible in agreement with the teachings of their own churches simply because they are the official teachings, or those most commonly accepted. Interpreters who do this are not really interpreting the Scripture passage, but accepting what others have taught.

Most evangelical Christians are emotionally attached to one specific system of eschatology—the doctrine of what will happen at the end of the present age—not because they have been able to draw conclusions from personal study but because their branch of the church or an esteemed teacher holds such a position. Many church people believe in "a proper way" to baptize, not because they find it to be true from the study of Scripture but because "my church teaches it that way."

In mentioning these examples of the dogmatic method of interpretation, we are not evaluating the truth of any particular doctrine but only demonstrating that *a method of interpretation has been used improperly* in reaching a conclusion.

The Grammatico—Historical Method

The right method will be the one that avoids the kind of errors mentioned above: a rationalism that will not admit the existence of the supernatural; any interpretation that does away with the historical reali-

ties described in the text and supplies allegorical or
mystical meanings; any dogmatism that insists on a
particular interpretation without taking into consideration the rules of hermeneutics that might point in another direction.

Such a method is called *grammatico-historical*. It
always requires that one interpret in agreement with
the characteristics of language, including the ones in
which the biblical text was written, as well as the language into which the Bible has been translated for the
reader. This approach regards the Bible to have been
written as true history; that is, neither allegorical, nor
composed of fables, legends, myths, traditions, de-
ceit, etc., except where the Scriptures themselves indicate that any passage is to be regarded in one of these
nonliteral senses.

This method is also the most ancient of all; its use
may be verified earlier than the second century after
Christ. While the Alexandrian theologians were using
the allegorical method in order to defend the Scriptures in their debates with pagans, the *literal method*
continued to be used in Antioch under Bishop Theophilus, who insisted on following the most ancient
practice of the Jews.[4]

The grammatico-historical method was known in
earliest times as *literal*. This term does not mean that
everything is to be interpreted literally, without recognizing the presence of literary figures, idioms, etc., but
that the *sense* is literal even though the language may
be figurative. Literal interpretation includes the use of
every kind of figurative language in a literal context.

---

[4]Philip Schaff, *History of the Christian Church*, vol. 1, 5th ed. (Grand
Rapids:Eerdmans, 1910), p. 816.

Literalism, on the other hand, usually forgets the proper use of literary figures in common speech.

Later, in the fourth century, Jerome abandoned his allegorical method in favor of the literal. Augustine moved toward the literal method but could never be completely in agreement with Jerome.

The reformers Luther and Calvin gave the principal impulse to the proper method through their emphasis on the original languages. These men demonstrated that the right understanding of the original languages of the Bible greatly clarified its true sense.

For Review

1. Name and describe briefly the three erroneous methods of interpretation, and tell why they are considered misleading.
2. How does the grammatico-historical method regard the Bible?

4

ACCURATE READING

On one of the television game shows a well-known comedian gave the wrong answer to a biblical question. According to the Bible, he said, a man has one less rib than a woman. When the master of ceremonies corrected him, he replied, "Somebody ought to tell the Man who wrote the Bible!"

Of course, the Bible makes no such statement (see Gen. 2:21–23). The television performer was mistaken due to reading the text carelessly, or perhaps to not reading it at all. In any case, he was like a vast number of people who draw conclusions about a text without checking carefully on their accuracy.

Bible readers may become so accustomed to its language that they read quickly over all-too-familiar words, thinking they are understanding exactly what the words say. Inattentive reading can reinforce errors in interpretation. To understand any written text correctly, it is always necessary to read it carefully. The more important the subject matter, the more serious will be the errors committed by failing to do so.

Sometimes we infer a mistaken idea from careless reading of a passage that obscures its true meaning. Many of us suppose that three wise men visited the

Christ Child shortly after His birth, but the account in Matthew does not mention how many there were (see Matt. 2:1–12). It is likely there were more than three, since the caravan in which they probably traveled would have been made up of many people. The idea that there were three wise men is undoubtedly derived from the mention of three kinds of gifts that were given to the infant King: gold, frankincense, and myrrh.

Another text that is often misquoted is 1 Timothy 6:10: "For the love of money is a root of all kinds of evil." It is commonly inferred that money itself is the root of all evil, probably because readers have not paid attention to all the words of the text, or because they have repeated the mistaken interpretation, which has become proverbial in the English language. It is, of course, the *love* of money that is called the root of evil. Nor is it the root of *all* evil, but a root of *all kinds* of evil. In these details, better translations of the text emphasize the true meaning of the original statement.

In his discussion of the body given to believers after death, in heaven, Paul wrote "Now He who has prepared us for this very thing is God, who also has given us the Spirit as a guarantee" (2 Cor. 5:5). I had always understood the text to say that God has prepared for us a habitation in heaven as a reward for the life we have lived here on earth, a consolation, as it were. One day I discovered that I had carelessly inverted the order of the words "us for." Only then did I realize that God has not prepared *heaven for us*, but *us for heaven*. Heaven is no consolation prize, but the great goal for which God is preparing us now by His Spirit.

Some readers have stumbled at 1 Corinthians 15:19: "If in this life only we have hope in Christ, we are of all men the most pitiable." The idea that may be mistakenly drawn from this verse is that if we have *only hope in Christ* in this life, we are most pitiable, as though our hope in Christ were not enough. Yet a careful reading of the verse will show that if our hope in Christ is only for this life, we are most pitiable; we hope in Christ for a resurrection to come.

When we say that it is necessary to read carefully, we mean (among other things) that we must understand and pay attention to the grammar of the text. Unfortunately, too many of us have an insufficient knowledge of grammar to be able to analyze the various elements of a sentence: nouns, verbs, adjectives, adverbs, pronouns, conjunctions, phrases, clauses, and so on. It will be well worth the time invested to study again the parts of speech and their functions in a sentence.

In 1 Corinthians 11:27 we find the apostle Paul's teaching about the significance of the Lord's Supper. He wrote:

Wherefore whosoever shall eat this bread, and drink this cup of the Lord, unworthily, shall be guilty of the body and blood of the Lord (KJV).

Many readers have understood the word "unworthily" to say that the unworthy believer should not take the Lord's Supper.

The text does not say that; if it did, none of us should partake of the Lord's Supper, for we are all unworthy before God. But if we note that "unworthily" is an adverb that refers to the manner in which the Supper is eaten, and not to the character of the believer, the difficulty is taken away. Notice the more accurate rendering of the New King James Version:

Therefore whoever eats this bread or drinks this cup of the Lord in an unworthy manner will be guilty of the body and blood of the Lord.

Paul is saying that the Supper is not to be observed in an unworthy manner, such as gluttony, drunkenness, disrespect, or eating in unbelief. According to verse 29, Paul's concern was that those who participate in the observance be able to "discern the body" of Christ.

Some versions of Scripture are based on a literal style of translation. The translators of the text tried to reproduce as much as possible the literal meaning and style of the original language. In some parts of the King James version, particularly in the writings of Paul, sentences are quite long and complicated. See, for example, Romans 5:10,12,15,17. The eight verses of Ephesians 1:3-10 are just two sentences, while verses 15-23 are only one. In the Good News Bible, the first group of verses in Ephesians is broken up into nine sentences, and the second group into seven.

Anyone who reads the King James Version or a similar translation must pay careful attention to the relationship between the elements of a sentence in order not to lose the precise meaning and train of thought. In the case of long, complicated sentences, read each phrase and clause as a part of the whole sentence, perhaps pausing after each grammatical unit in order to capture the meaning of the text.

Still, the older, more literal translations are a distinct help in showing how the original reads, i.e., what it says. Some of the more modern, freer translations help the reader understand what the text means. In this sense, the latter are more like commentaries than exact translations and may suggest a mistaken idea in any particular place.

The rule, then, is that in order to interpret the Scriptures properly, we must always read carefully, taking into account the grammatical structure of the text. This principle implies the use of a clear and accurate translation, one in which the translators have taken care to express themselves with grammatical clarity and exactness.

For Review

1. Did all living creatures on earth die in the flood? Did the fish die along with the rest of the animal life? (Gen. 6:7; 7:3).
2. Is it true in an unlimited sense that "the truth shall make you free" as Jesus said? (John 8:31–32).
3. Can a man do anything, according to the expression "I can do all things" in Philippians 4:13?
4. According to Genesis 38:9–10, what was the sin of Onan? See the reason why he did what he did.

5
THE MEANING OF INDIVIDUAL WORDS

Everyone who has ever studied a foreign language is keenly aware of the pitfalls of translation. During President Carter's visit to Poland in 1977, his highly paid translator represented him as saying: "When I abandoned the United States," instead of "When I left the United States." Fortunately the mistake drew only a snicker from the crowd. In Taiwan, the Pepsi slogan "Come alive with Pepsi" was turned into the claim that "Pepsi brings your ancestors back from the dead." And the General Motors slogan "Body by Fisher" was translated in several countries as "Corpse by Fisher."[1]

These illustrations point up the fact that words do not always translate readily. While most words have their recognized translations in other languages, it is safe to say that there are no perfect equivalents. Each word has its own "area of meaning," which is not identical with the area of meaning in any other language.

In English, "coach" may have any of the following meanings: a horse-drawn carriage, a perambulator, a railroad car, or an athletic instructor. But its equiva-

---

[1]"Ignorance of Language Threatens U.S. Interests," (Columbia, S.C.) *The State*, 3 Dec. 1980.

lent in Spanish, *coche*, may mean a taxi, a private automobile, a pushcart, and in parts of Mexico and Central America, a pig. But the area of meaning common to both languages includes the principle idea of a conveyance of some kind. This is what allows the word to be translated easily in most cases.

In the same way, the words used to translate the Bible into English do not always represent the exact sense of the original words; nor do they include all that the original words meant in the biblical language. It is therefore important to know as completely as possible what the words meant in the Greek or Hebrew in order to understand properly the meaning of many texts.

Putting this into practice, however, is not very easy since few students have had the opportunity or time to study the biblical languages. Happily there are a variety of reference works available in libraries and bookstores to help with this need.

One of the most useful references is the concordance, designed to locate particular texts by word or topic. Concordances also give a great deal of help in comparative word studies. James Strong's *Exhaustive Concordance* and Robert Young's *Analytical Concordance* are both excellent and widely used. In addition to concordances, there are more specialized aids in the field of language study. These include Greek and Hebrew lexicons, expository dictionaries, and wordbooks. For a full list of Bible study resources see "Suggested Books for the Bible Student" on page 216.

An example of the need to know original meanings is seen in Jesus' command: "Repent, and believe in the gospel" (Mark 1:15). Many readers have the idea that repentance means sorrow for sin. The English word "repent" does not itself give us a clear idea of the meaning of the original Greek word. The word *meta-noeō* is composed of two elements: *meta*, a preposition indicating a change; and *noeō*, to think. Together, the elements signify a change of mind; in the biblical usage, *a change of mind with regard to sin and/or God*.

Phillips's translation says, "Change your hearts and minds," while the Living Bible says, "Turn from your sins." A popular Spanish translation says boldly: "Return to God." Note that these translators found it necessary to translate by means of a phrase instead of a single word.

Another case where the usual translation is inadequate is in Ephesians 6:14: "Stand therefore . . . having put on the breastplate of righteousness." Almost every English version translates the Greek word *thōraka* as "breastplate," one part of the old Roman armor. Only the New English Bible uses "coat of mail." This is undoubtedly the best. Otherwise, the point could be made that when Christians turn their backs, they have no protection with only a breastplate for cover. This was certainly not true of the Roman soldier; he had protection completely around his body. Thayer's Greek lexicon gives the meaning of the word *thōraka* as "a breastplate or corselet, consisting of two parts and protecting the body on both sides from the neck to the middle." Knowing the full meaning of the word in the original language, as found in a Greek lexicon, gives an extra dimension to the verse. More importantly, the interpreter should note that Paul was talking primarily about righteousness, of which the breastplate or coat of mail is only a figure.

Many such words may be better understood by

investigating their origin or composition, known as their "etymology," but Mickelsen reminds us that such investigations require caution. For example, the word "enthusiasm" has its origins in the Latin and Greek. Until fairly recently it meant "to be possessed by a god" and had the sense of supernatural inspiration and prophetic and poetic ecstasy. However, now it means only a strong excitement of feeling, ardent zeal in any pursuit.[2]

A biblical example is found in Romans 8:26, which says that the Holy Spirit intercedes for us "with groanings which cannot be uttered." This seems like a contradiction; how can we call something that remains unuttered a "groaning"? But the real key lies in the Greek word *stenagmois*, here translated as "groanings." A Greek lexicon shows that *stenagmois* may also mean "sighings." A "sighing" is not uttered; in fact, it can scarcely be heard. Also, "sighing" better fits the context, since Paul is discussing how a Christian asks for something he deeply desires; "sighing" would convey that sense of longing, while "groaning" seems to imply pain or anxiety.

Some words, even though they are correctly translated, lack the force in English they had in the common speech of the Greeks. It was the connotation or shared cultural background of those words that gave them their special meaning in the original.

A case in point is the familiar statement in Romans 6:23: "The wages of sin is death." The word translated "wages" is *opsōnia* in Greek, and was used of the wages paid to soldiers, or of the rations given them in place of a salary. In those days the soldiers' wages

---

[2]Mickelsen, *Interpreting the Bible*, p. 6.

were miserable, both in quantity and quality (see Luke 3:14). This idea is completely lacking in our present translations. The text could well be rendered: "the miserable salary of sin is death."

We should note also that many words used in the New Testament were used in a special or limited sense, according to the geographical area where they were used, or the particular time in history. We call that sense the "local usage" or, in technical jargon, the *usus loquendi.* It is advisable to investigate and learn to what extent the words, both in English and in Greek, were affected by the time and place in which they were used.

In the seventeenth century when the Bible was translated by English scholars during the reign of King James, the English word "love" had a vulgar, sensuous connotation. When they translated 1 Corinthians 13, they used the word "charity" for the familiar Greek word *agapē.* The local usage of the word "love" would not permit its use in any sublime context. Today the word *love* is vague and general enough to permit this usage, while *charity* carries the specific sense of a benevolent contribution.

A similar thing may be noted in the use of the word "prevent" in 1 Thessalonians 4:15: "we which are alive . . . shall not prevent them which are asleep," (KJV). In King James' day it meant "precede" or "go ahead of" and was a good choice for the translators. In modern usage it means "stop" or "withhold."

The "begats" of Genesis and Matthew have little meaning for the modern reader. Almost unanimously our present-day translations use the phrase "was the father of," rather than use another awkward word like "engendered."

The word "baptize" is a term derived from the

Greek that appears in the languages of many translations. In the days when many translations were being
produced in Europe, there were serious debates over
the original meaning of the Greek word *baptizō* and
the most appropriate way to translate it. Skirting the
issue, the translators adopted the plan of *transliter-
ating* rather than translating the word; they merely
adapted the word to a suitable form in every language
of translation. The result is that the word "baptize"
does not help us to know the meaning of the original,
because it is essentially the same word.

No one debates the fact that the literal meaning of
the word is to immerse or submerge. For Baptists,
some Mennonites, the Churches of Christ, various
Pentecostal groups, many Methodists, and the whole
Eastern Orthodox Church, the meaning is immersion.
Others insist that the word *baptizō* meant "to dye
cloth" as well as "to immerse." This agrees with another clear meaning of the word, "to dip repeatedly."
These people hold that Christian baptism symbolized
the "new color" given to the believer through the work
of the Holy Spirit. They feel that sprinkling, pouring,
or chrismating can represent new life in Christ as well
as immersion can.

Still another meaning for the word "baptize" is to be
found in Mark 7:4:"And there are many other things
. . . like the washing of cups, pitchers, copper vessels,
and couches." Many ancient manuscripts add the
word "couches" or "beds" to this verse, as noted in the
American Standard Version. The Jews sprinkled,
washed, or "baptized" many things in a ceremonial
manner. But it would be most unlikely that they im-
mersed their beds for this purpose. Consequently,
most translators translate *baptizō* as "wash."

The Bible interpreter must use the results of the best

studies available, in order to determine what the meaning of a word is and whether it ever has another meaning in certain contexts. The interpreter should be aware that such questions are not usually settled through the use of a single interpretive principle, but with the help of all principles that may have a bearing on the subject.

Some words have a special use in the Bible text that must be determined through the study of the various passages where they are found. A concordance will be the most helpful tool in finding these passages. Often a single word will have different meanings, according to the way it is used, and it will not be immediately clear in which of the various senses the writer has used it.

For example, the word "law" is used in many ways. It may have any one of the following meanings: (1) the five books of Moses, (2) all the writings of the Old Testament, (3) the Ten Commandments, (4) the civil law of any nation, (5) the inborn power of sin, (6) the principle of law in contrast with the principle of grace, and perhaps others.

In the same way, words such as *flesh, world, gospel, spirit, death, righteousness, fear, soul, heart, faith, light,* and others do not always have the same meaning throughout Scripture.

Some very important New Testament words do not portray exactly what they meant to their pagan Greek users. A study of these words shows that their original meaning has been adapted to the needs of Christian doctrine.

For example, the word "church," translated from the Greek word *ekklēsia,* is used in the New Testament to mean the congregation of God, and especially of those who believe in Jesus Christ. In common usage

among the Greeks, the word meant the assembly of
the people of the ancient city-states in a pure democratic form of government. Every citizen was "called
out" to a public meeting to take part in the affairs of
government. It is from the verb "to call out," *ek-kaleō*,
that *ekklēsia* is derived. Jesus used the word to describe His church, if He spoke in Greek.[3] In any case,
the word *ekklēsia* should be studied together with its
Hebrew equivalent, *qahal*. Since the time when Jesus
used it to describe His people, *ekklēsia* has been used
in this special sense in the New Testament, which is
quite different from the way the Greeks used it.

In this case, the etymology of the word is useful. But
Mickelsen urges us not to insist that Christians are
"called-out ones" in the sense that they are called out
from the world by God's election.[4] While that is true in
itself, the word *ekklēsia* is not used with this intent.

In a similar way, the words *baptism, regeneration,
justification* and *salvation* took on new meanings
through their use among Christians and in the New
Testament. The word "love," *agapē*, had a rather
limited use among the Greeks; but among Christians it
took on a meaning almost original.

Among the ancient people, personal names had a
special, private meaning, which often affects the interpretation of the texts where they are used. The
name Noah meant "rest." He is described in Genesis
6:9 as a man without faults, and as "the only good
man of his time" (GNB). Without a doubt, his father
Lamech gave him that name in the expectation that he

---

[3]Whether Jesus spoke in Greek or Aramaic is not absolutely certain; the
evidence seems to be on the side of Aramaic. In that case He would have
used the Hebrew term *qahal*, translated in the Septuagint as *ekklēsia* (Ps.
22:22). This is the same Greek word found in Hebrews 2:12.

[4]Mickelsen, *Interpreting the Bible*, p. 121.

would have a son that would give rest to his own spirit in the midst of a perverse world; happily it turned out that way.

Adam was called by that name because he was man; Eve got her name from the fact that she was to be the mother of all people (Gen. 3:20). Naomi's name means pleasant; but she protested against it and asked to be called Marah, because "the Almighty has dealt very bitterly with me" (Ruth 1:20). Marah means bitter. In many places knowing the meaning of an individual's name helps us understand the passage.

It is an exaggeration to say that no one should interpret the Bible without a thorough knowledge of its original languages, but the interpreter should form the habit of investigating the original meaning of the words in the texts being studied. Frequently the key to understanding them will be found through that study.

For Review

1. Apart from the reference books mentioned in this chapter, what obvious source will give the meaning of words found in the English Bible?
2. Study the following texts and determine the meaning of the word "law" in each case: Esther 1:8; Psalm 19:7–8; Matthew 5:18; 7:12; Romans 2:12; 7:2; 7:23; Galatians 3:11; 5:23; James 1:25.
3. In Genesis 6:9, how is the word "perfect" to be understood?
4. In Genesis 24:16 Rebecca is described as a virgin. Why does the writer add "neither had any man known her"? Isn't that the meaning of "virgin"?

6
THE CONTEXT

You may have heard of the lady who loved the Bible because it was "full of such nice quotations." Many people read the Bible that way, hoping to find one of those quotable verses. These readers ignore the setting in which the verses are found and give the impression that it is made up of meaningless or difficult words. Naturally, that kind of reading leads to a great deal of misunderstanding. The connection of those choice verses with the setting in which they appear is what gives them their true meaning.

Even preachers have been known to use verses that appear on the surface to supply an excellent sermon text. The most unbelievable case I ever heard was when a pastor of an earlier generation used a few words from Matthew 24:17 to preach against the custom of the ladies of his congregation who wore their hair in "topnots." ("Let him . . . on the housetop not come down" KJV.) He took his text from the words "top not come down." This case was reported as fact by one of my professors; except for that, I would doubt that anyone could so violently twist the meaning of the words and evade the context of the phrase.

On another occasion an atheist asserted to me that

"the Bible says there is no God." He may have never read Psalm 14:1 for himself, because he was not happy to learn that the verse really says: *"The fool has said in his heart,/'There is no God' "* (italics mine).

Disregarding the surrounding text is perhaps the most common error in biblical interpretation, and perhaps the easiest to correct. But it will require an openness of mind and the willingness to reject whatever false interpretation may have been put on the "nice quotation" in question. It is always necessary to note carefully the words that precede and follow a particular verse. Those words are called the *context*, because they are found in close connection with (Latin, *con*) the text. The context may be either *immediate* or more *remote*, but it will always have a bearing on the meaning.

The Immediate Context

Let us examine several passages that can be easily misunderstood apart from their immediate context. In Genesis 18:12 Sarah laughs and says in her heart: "After I have grown old, shall I have pleasure, my lord being old also?" Seeing the verse by itself suggests that Sarah referred to the pleasure of sexual intercourse. Both the Good News Bible and the Living Bible support this interpretation. But a careful reading of the context (vv. 11,13) shows that the pleasure referred to is *childbearing*. Abraham was not so old that he could not have sexual intercourse, because after Sarah's death he remarried and gave Keturah, his second wife, six sons (Gen. 25:1–2).

Ecclesiastes 1:9 apparently teaches that "there is nothing new under the sun," passing over the fact that there may be many new things in human affairs. The context indicates that the writer was speaking of the natural world and of corrupt human nature. (see vv. 2–11).

Still another case of misinterpretation as a result of ignoring the context may be seen in 1 Corinthians 2:9: "Eye has not seen, nor ear heard,/Nor have entered into the heart of man/The things which God has prepared for those who love Him." This text is often quoted as though it spoke of the wonderful things God has prepared for us in heaven, things we cannot now understand. But the surrounding verses show that Paul is speaking of Old Testament times, *before the coming of the gospel* as we know it. In verse 8 we read that the rulers of this world crucified Jesus because they did not know who He was. In verse 10 Paul contrasts that former ignorance with the new insight given to Christians through the Spirit: "But God has revealed them to us. . . ." The text does not refer to the things of heaven yet to come, but to the mysteries of the gospel now made clear to believers.

Often the context of a particular verse has an important bearing on Christian theology. Hebrews 7:12 declares that: "For the priesthood being changed, of necessity there is also a change of the law." Some theologians use this as a proof text to show that there has been a change in the Mosaic Law concerning the priesthood, which allows others who are not Jews to serve as priests. The immediate context (7:13–18; 8:1–2) teaches that the change of law was the prophesied ministry of Christ as the eternal High Priest in place of the Aaronic priesthood authorized by the Mosaic Law. Christ does away with the whole institution of the priesthood, rather than establish a new order of priests (see 8:6–13 and 13:10,15).

The Remote Context

Just as it is necessary to examine any text in its own immediate context, it is also necessary to consider the remote context—to compare it with the general teaching of the Bible. For example, Ecclesiastes 9:5 is used in support of the doctrines of "soul-sleep" and "annihilation" of the soul: "For the living know that they will die; But the dead know nothing." Taken by itself, the verse seems to say that there is no consciousness after death. But the remote context shows that this interpretation is contradictory and false, and the remote context of the Book of Ecclesiastes itself shows the writer was speaking only with regard to present, physical life: The dead "know nothing" *about this life.* This agrees with the whole view of the writer of Ecclesiastes.

Many of the Proverbs are isolated statements of wisdom; they have no immediate context. But their truth should be weighed against other statements of Scripture and the general tone of biblical teaching. This is the remote context of those isolated teachings of wisdom.

Often the leaders of heretical sects base their doctrines on texts which, in isolation, seem to say things of a contrary nature. Followers of these leaders do not understand the general teaching of the Bible on those subjects, nor consider how unreasonable it is to accept those special doctrines apart from the Bible's teaching as a whole. To do so is like accepting the testimony of a single witness against the united voice of all other witnesses.

Biblically oriented Christians believe that the Author of Scripture was the Holy Spirit and that the Bible

contains no real contradictions. Every part of Scripture is in complete harmony with every other part
when it is rightly interpreted.

This point of view is not a device for avoiding the
difficulties of apparent contradictions, nor is it evidence of a closed mind. When there are genuine problems, an impartial study is required before passing
judgment on a doubtful text.

There are numerous examples of the need to examine the teaching of the whole Bible.

Psalm 51:5 has been misinterpreted to become the
source of an erroneous doctrine. According to the
older versions of Scripture, David wrote: "Behold . . .
in sin my mother conceived me." If the reader fails to
compare this with other teachings in the Bible, he is
likely to think that cohabitation, the sexual contact
between the parents of David, was sin. For this reason
some believe and teach that marriage is an inferior
spiritual state to celibacy, and that sexual intercourse
can be sin even in marriage.

This is not what the Bible teaches in other places. In
Genesis 1:28 God says to Adam and Eve: "Be fruitful,
and multiply; fill the earth. . . ." Then in 2:24 we read:
"Therefore a man shall leave his father and mother
and be joined to his wife, and they shall become one
flesh." Again, in Hebrews 13:4 we read: "Marriage is
honorable among all, and the bed undefiled; but forni-
cators and adulterers God will judge." The teaching of
the whole Bible contradicts the idea that sexual intercourse, within the marriage bond, is sin.

Then what is the proper way to understand Psalm
51:5? In the first place we should never use a doubtful
text as the basis for any doctrine, especially when the
Bible as a whole teaches something very different. As

we read Psalm 51, we see that it is a confession of sin. Verses 1 to 4 speak of David's sin; and in verse 5 he confesses that his sin existed from the time of his birth, even since his conception. It should be clear that the sin to which he refers is not that of his parents but his own. The Living Bible and the Good News Bible give this sense, as does the New International Version: "Surely I have been a sinner from birth, sinful from the time my mother conceived me."

Faith vs. Works

It has often been said that the theology of Paul and James is in conflict. James is said to teach that the justification of the sinner depends equally upon faith and works, while Paul insists that faith is the only basis for justification (see Rom. 3:21–22). Those who support this view quote James 2:24: "You see then that a man is justified by works, and not by faith only."

There is no real contradiction here. James is saying that faith, *by itself*, is dead, that is, faith without any works to validate it, is dead. He says exactly this in verse 26: "For as the body without the spirit is dead, so faith without works is dead." The faith James insists upon is faith like that of Abraham (v. 23) and Rahab (v. 25); it is faith that leads one to do right. We may not say that it is faith plus works that justifies a person, but rather faith that produces works is the faith that justifies. In this way we see that there is no contradiction in the teaching of these two writers of Scripture; rather they complement one another.

Eternal Punishment

There are those who refuse to accept the biblical teaching of eternal punishment for sin after death. In support of their view they quote Ecclesiastes 6:6: "Even if he lives a thousand years twice over—but has not seen goodness. *Do not all go to one place?*" It sounds to the casual reader as though all men go to the same place after death, and that there is no distinction as to the reward or punishment they receive. Clearly, the Bible teaches the very opposite; otherwise it would have no message concerning life after death.

The problem is solved by understanding that the writer of Ecclesiastes was not speaking about the destiny of the soul but of the physical body. All people die and have the grave as their common destiny. The writer said merely that this present life ends at death.

Salvation

From the reading of texts such as Acts 2:40, "Be saved from this perverse generation"; 1 Timothy 4:16, "You will save both yourself and those who hear you"; and James 5:20, "He who turns a sinner . . . will save a soul from death," one might conclude that salvation is largely the work of man. But such a conclusion would fly in the face of the teaching of the rest of the Bible. Those texts merely reflect the fact that we have a part to play in God's saving work; we must respond to God's mercy through Christ's sacrificial death in order to be saved.

In general, the books of the Bible are bound together by the theme of God's redemption of man. This internal unity supplies the context for all of the Bible's parts. This context must always be considered in the interpretation of any biblical text.

For Review

1. Genesis 4:17 apparently teaches that Cain found his wife "in the land of Nod." Who was she and where did he get her? After thinking about it, read Genesis 5:4 and make a statement.
2. Mark 16:16 seems to teach that baptism is necessary for salvation. Is this the teaching of the New Testament? See 1 Corinthians 1:14–17.
3. According to Luke 15:7 it appears that repentance is not necessary in order to be saved. How should this verse be understood?
4. Is it possible to buy one's way to heaven? How is Luke 16:9 to be understood?
5. Examine and interpret the following texts in the light of their context: 1 Corinthians 2:9 (see vv. 6–8); Matthew 24:32 (see vv. 26–31,33); Ephesians 5:22 (see vv. 21, 25–33); Colossians 2:21 (see vv. 20, 22, 23).

7

PARALLEL
PASSAGES

One of my children once asked me: "Why do some of the books of the Bible tell the same thing about Jesus?" She had noticed what Bible readers have often realized: that there are four Gospels, and that in many places they tell the same story, frequently using identical language.

Of course, there are many places where the stories are not identical, even though the similarities convince the reader that the same story is being presented in different Gospels. In most cases the variant forms of the account throw additional light on the event and help the reader understand more completely what happened.

Bible passages that refer to the same subject are called "parallel passages." The expression is also used of portions of Scripture that deal with the same laws, doctrines, or prophecies, using similar language.

In the study of any passage of the Bible whose subject is treated in other passages, it will be necessary to examine all those passages in order to get the whole teaching. Any interpretation that fails to do this will be inadequate. In some cases the failure to read the parallel passage will result in serious error.

New Testament Parallels

There are cases where a careful comparison of the parallel passages will help resolve inconsistencies that arise from the reading of the different accounts. In Matthew 9:18, 23-26, we find the first reference to the raising of Jairus's daughter from the dead. In verse 18, Matthew records that Jairus says his daughter "has just died." But in Mark 5:23 Jairus says that she is "at the point of death." We ask ourselves which was the case: was she dead, or was she only dying at this point? Luke supports Mark's words, saying that "she was dying" (Luke 8:42).

When we weigh the various statements we are impressed with the thought that Jairus's words according to Matthew indicate primarily the intensity of his concern; he was in anguish. Since she had been dying or was at the point of death when he left home, his anxiety convinced him that in the meantime she had already died. Hence, "My daughter has just died." This insight into Jairus's state of mind lends additional interest to the story.

The study of parallel passages allows a more complete understanding of any event. In Matthew 9:2-8 we find the story of the healing of a paralyzed man who was taken to Jesus on a pallet by some friends. In Mark 2:2-12 we are told that the sick man was carried by four men and that they lowered him through the roof, where they had made an opening. In Luke 5:17-26 we learn that the roof was made of tile, and thus the opening they made probably did no damage.[1] Taken together, the various details provide the reader

---

[1]The verb used in Mark, *apestégasan*, uncovered, may be used in two ways: to remove the roof, or to break it up. It does not necessarily mean that the roof was of mud. Here it should be understood in agreement with what Luke states, that it was of tile.

a rather full description of what happened, without resorting to imagination. Unless the parallel passages are studied closely, the Bible teacher may contradict one of the other Gospels.

There are three very important passages, dealing with the deity of Christ: Colossians 1:15-19; Hebrews 1:1-3; and Revelation 1:4-8. These may be regarded as parallel passages because they deal with the same subject, and they all affirm that Christ existed before the earth or anything else was created.

There are those who insist that since Jesus Christ is the "firstborn over all creation" (Col. 1:15), He is not the Creator but that He was created first in the creative process, the first among all created beings. The expression taken by itself seems to bear out that interpretation. But a careful study of this passage reveals that the word "firstborn" refers, in this place, to the predecessor of creation, not to the first of a series of creations. Phillips renders the expression this way: "He existed before creation began." The New English Bible says: "His is the primacy over all created things." The Good News Bible reads: "He is the firstborn Son, superior to all created beings." The reader should observe that the following verse sets forth the same truth: "For by him all things were created" (v. 16). Here He is described as the Creator Himself. The parallel passages in Hebrews and Revelation confirm this teaching, lest we be confused.

When all four Gospels appear to be at variance with each other, one is tempted to question the accuracy of any of them. This is the case with the four different wordings of the sign above Jesus' cross. According to Matthew 27:37 the sign read: THIS IS JESUS THE KING OF THE JEWS. Mark reports it in its shortest form: THE KING OF THE JEWS (15:26). Luke 23:38

has THIS IS THE KING OF THE JEWS, and John 19:19 gives this version: JESUS OF NAZARETH, THE KING OF THE JEWS.

The only words common to the four are KING OF THE JEWS. Matthew and John include the name of Jesus, while Matthew and Luke agree that the sign began with THIS IS . . . . Mark's report is the shortest; he wrote the shortest Gospel. Only John mentions Nazareth as the place of His origin.

How may we resolve this discrepancy?

Some commentators explain the different forms of the title as being translations of the three languages in which it was written: Hebrew, Latin, and Greek. In each of the languages the length of the title would be different: Hebrew uses fewer letters, Latin omits the articles, and Greek would give the title in the longest form. Some adjustment of the titles on the sign board would be necessary to make them fit in the same space.

This explanation has much in its favor, but it is impossible to know from which language each of the Evangelists reported the title, or for that matter, whether this is the correct explanation. It may be better to suppose that each Gospel writer used the title that best suited his purposes, though for reasons unknown to us. But if our curiosity demands it, we may judge that the total information given on the title board may be gathered from the four Gospel reports, as follows:

MATTHEW:	This is Jesus	The King of the Jews
MARK:	. . . .	The King of the Jews
LUKE:	This is	The King of the Jews
JOHN:	. . . . Jesus of Nazareth	The King of the Jews

THIS IS JESUS OF NAZARETH THE KING OF THE JEWS

In one language or another, this is probably what the title said. Each of the Gospel writers has given us only a part of the information. This fact will supply one of the answers to the question: Why do we have four Gospels? Since human testimonies are generally incomplete, we need all four to get the fullest possible account of the facts.

Another helpful study from three of the Gospels is the Lord's prediction of Peter's denial the night before the crucifixion, and the way it was accomplished *as reported in each Gospel.* The prediction is found in Matthew 26:34, Mark 14:30, and John 13:38. The fulfillment is found in Matthew 26:69–75, Mark 14:66–72, and John 18:16,17,25–27. The student will notice that each fulfillment agrees with the way the prediction is stated in the same Gospel.

One problem that arises from the study is this: Why does Mark write that the cock was to crow twice, while the other two speak only of the cock crowing once?

My suggestion here is not intended to be dogmatic. But it is a fact known to anyone who lives on a farm, that when the rooster crows, he crows several times, then stops for a while, then crows again several times. Each of these cock-crowings is a multiple event, not a single "cock-a-doodle-doo." It is possible, then, that Matthew and John thought of the cock-crowing with this in mind: "Before the rooster crows twice, you will deny Me three times" (Mark 14:30).

Old Testament Parallels

In the study of the books of Samuel, Kings, and Chronicles, it will often be helpful to study parallel passages that deal with the same history. The books of Ezra and Nehemiah do not record the same events, but each does contain details that supply a helpful commentary on the other. (The same is true of the Book of the Acts and the Epistles of Paul.) Certain of the Psalms should be studied in connection with the historical event associated with their composition. This is sometimes indicated in the titles at the head of the various Psalms. Not all of them, however, tell on what occasion they were composed.

In the study of some Old Testament passages, the New Testament texts related to them should be examined. Sometimes the New Testament interpretation does not seem to agree with the original history.

For example, the story of Moses striking the Egyptian and killing him (Ex. 2:11–15) represents Moses as a murderer who flees from Pharaoh. Stephen, however, mentions that event as part of God's plan for sending Moses as the liberator of his people (Acts 7:23–35). Undoubtedly both aspects of that story should be kept in mind as we interpret the life of Moses.

In the story of Lot (Gen. 13 and 19) we see him as a man without a very deep spiritual life and lacking good judgment. But the apostle Peter calls him "righteous Lot" (2 Pet. 2:7–8), and tells us that he "was oppressed with the filthy conduct of the wicked" and that he "tormented his righteous soul from day to day by seeing and hearing their lawless deeds." These are two very different views of the man, and both should affect our understanding of this Old Testament figure.

In some cases an interpretation based on a detail that does not appear in all of the parallel passages is emphasized more than it should be. The fig tree mentioned in Matthew 24:32 is often considered to be a symbol of Israel. The verse is explained by some commentators to mean that when the branch of the fig tree grows tender—that is, when Israel begins to lean toward faith in Christ—then the coming of Christ is near.

A comparison with Luke 21:29 will show that the Lord did not speak of the fig tree as a symbol of Israel, but as the most common tree of the land. We know this because Jesus said "Look at the fig tree, and all the trees." The trees were not *all* symbols of Israel. The lesson in this parable is that the trees become tender and put forth leaves as a sign that summer is near. In the same way, when the events mentioned in the earlier part of the chapter take place, believers may know that Christ's coming is at hand.

Prophetic books or passages that speak of the same period of future or past history should be studied together. Any one of their passages may be the best commentary on the prophecies being studied in another book. For example, the prophecy of Daniel 7:2-8 may be studied profitably along with that of Revelation 13:1-2.

When we remember that the Bible has doctrinal unity, and that there are no real contradictions among its various parts, we will better understand how important it is to examine all parallel passages and every historical circumstance that has any bearing on the subject being studied.

The most practical way to apply this rule will be to use a Bible with cross-references, a concordance, and one's own memory. The student should try to become familiar with Bible content so that those passages that are related come to mind easily.

For Review

1. Study each of the parallel passages that contain the prophecy of Peter's denial of Christ and the way it actually occurred according to each Gospel.
2. Study the life of King Solomon, especially 1 Kings 11:1–13. Why does Jesus mention Solomon as a wise man?

8
THE HISTORICAL BACKGROUND

During the years I spent in ministry among the Aztec Indians of Mexico, word came one day that one of the Indian believers had fallen away. He reportedly had said I taught that it was acceptable for a man to marry his sister!

Then I remembered an earlier conversation: he had asked me where Cain got his wife. On the basis of Genesis 5:4, I said she was undoubtedly his sister. I had tried to tell this new Christian that everyone in that day had descended from the first couple, Adam and Eve. But the Indian had failed to grasp the historical situation and concluded that what was necessary or acceptable in earlier time should be continued today.

From time to time we may find passages whose full meaning escapes us, even though the basic thrust of the words is clear. Understanding the historical background often clarifies such texts. This includes the customs and manners, the laws and philosophy of the people of the Bible, their history, geography, legends, art and crafts, tools, and everything that makes up the culture of a given time and place.

Such background information will be found principally in reference books dealing with ancient times. Bible dictionaries, encyclopedias, handbooks, and histories are the most helpful, but commentaries and archaeological studies are also useful. Both the Bible student and teacher will want to acquire several texts of this kind, including books on the daily life of the Jews, such as the various writings of Alfred Edersheim, their traditional laws found in the Talmud, and their history, including both the Old Testament and the books of the Apocrypha.[1] A list of study resources is found under "Suggested Books for the Bible Student" (see p. 216).

The following passages illustrate the way in which the understanding of historical backgrounds contributes to proper interpretation. Rachel's advice to Jacob may puzzle or offend us: "Here is my maid Bilhah; go in to her, and she will bear a child on my knees, that I also may have children by her" (Gen. 30:3). We will remember that Sarah, too, asked Abraham to take her servant Hagar for the same reason. Even though the patriarchs and their wives had settled in Canaan, they still followed this perfectly legal practice of the city of Ur. Because of the influence of that great city, the custom was recognized and accepted in much of the ancient world.

Again, in Genesis 31:19 we read that "Rachel had stolen the household idols that were her father's," and we wonder why. It would appear that she wanted to continue to worship the gods of her father Laban. However, this hardly explains why Laban was so

---

[1]The Talmud is the Jewish oral tradition, written down only several centuries after the beginning of the Christian era. The Apocrypha includes the works of Jewish history and mythology, written during the four centuries immediately before Christ. These books were not accepted by the Jews as canonical; only the Roman Catholic church recognizes them as authoritative.

angry. Why would he pursue Jacob and his family for the sake of a few small clay images?

But the household idols were not necessarily images. This word included any objects associated with the home. In ancient times the household idols were very much like the title deed to one's house and lands; the one who possessed them could claim the property.[2] It would appear that Rachel's theft was not motivated by a spirit of idolatry, but in the hope that she might claim Laban's property at a later date. He had taken nearly everything that belonged to Jacob and Rachel (see Gen. 31: 14–16). Of course, Jacob did not know what Rachel had done and never considered taking possession of Laban's property.

In Deuteronomy 27:11–14 we read that Moses commanded half the people to stand on Mount Gerizim and bless the nation. The other half were to stand on Mount Ebal to pronounce a curse, speaking "with a loud voice." One wonders how they could speak loudly enough to be heard and understood from one mountain to another. Even when we know that a shout in the mountains may be heard a long way off, it is not easy to understand the words.

However, a study of the topography of the land will show that the mountains were close enough to allow a voice to be heard from one mountainside to the other. And when we consider that the voice was not that of a single individual but of a large multitude speaking in concert and in a loud voice, we perceive that the blessing and the curse could be easily understood, especially since the message of each group was known in advance.

A similar circumstance is seen in Judges 9:7 where

[2]Henry S. Gehman, ed., *The New Westminster Dictionary of the Bible* (Philadelphia: Westminster, 1970), p. 936.

we read that "Jotham . . . stood on top of Mount Gerizim, and lifted his voice," and called to the people
below. In this case we wonder how a single voice
could be heard and understood from the top of the
mountain. It turns out that Gerizim forms a peak not
very high above the town of Shechem and contains an
outcropping of rock where Jotham may have stood
when he spoke. So again, the text may be resolved by
knowing something of the topography of the area.

In some cases the Old Testament itself holds the
explanation of certain points in the gospel history. In
Matthew 13:44, we read this parable: "Again, the
kingdom of heaven is like treasure hidden in a field,
which a man found and hid; and for joy over it he goes
and sells all that he has and buys that field." In our
opinion the man's conduct is somewhat questionable:
He bought the field so he could claim the treasure he
had found. We may feel that he should have gone to
the owner of the field and turned the treasure over to
him or, at least, told him about it.

However, the Jews did not hold our present viewpoint. Treasures were the property of those who
found them (see Job 3:21 and Prov. 2:4). Whenever
anyone was fortunate enough to find a long-hidden
treasure, no one begrudged him the right to claim it as
his own.

Of course, the parable was told with the principal
aim of emphasizing the great value of the gospel message, which is compared to a hidden treasure, and to
show how crucial it is to take for oneself the message
of salvation.

The case of the disciples' breaking off the ripened
heads of grain to satisfy their hunger raises a similar
problem of ethics: "And His disciples were hungry,

and began to pluck heads of grain and to eat" (Matt. 12:1). Was it right to take and eat what belonged to someone else? Wasn't this a case of petty theft? The text itself deals only with the violation of the sabbath day.

According to the law of Moses (Deut. 23:25) this practice was specifically permitted. The hungry traveler or stranger could pluck the grain and eat it, even though he was forbidden to harvest it. That provision in the law was made in the public interest, in recognition of the social obligations and spiritual values of the Hebrew nation. Jesus and His disciples did not commit any fault by eating the grain, nor did their critics mention theft in their accusation.

Jewish customs often explain even stranger things. In Luke 10, we read about the sending of the Seventy to preach the gospel, and Jesus' instructions regarding their travels. In verse 4 He says: "greet no one along the road."

It may seem strange to us that the Lord should have required such an antisocial attitude in the preaching of the gospel. However, Jewish greetings were very lengthy. When they met on the road, the Jews would greet each other with a slow *Shalom* (peace), bowing low to the right, from the waist. Then they repeated the greeting, bowing to the left. After this they politely discussed the affairs of the day, and on separating, repeated the *Shalom*. Such greetings often lasted a half an hour or more.

It is easy to imagine the effect of this custom on one's time, especially when there was some urgency. The meaning of Jesus' words in verse 4 is simply that His messengers were not to waste time. A specific example of this in Israel's earlier history is seen in

Elisha's command to his servant. He was to hurry to the house of the widow and lay his staff on the face of the dead child (2 Kin. 4:29); he was to greet no one, nor answer if he was saluted.

Another case involving the strange customs of the Jews is found in Matthew 8:21. One potential follower of Jesus wanted to postpone his obedience to the Lord's call with what appeared to be a legitimate excuse: "Lord, let me first go and bury my father." But Jesus replied, "Follow Me, and let the dead bury their own dead."

It is clear that Jesus was speaking figuratively in saying that the dead should bury their own dead; He was speaking of those who were spiritually dead. But the main problem is understanding why Jesus did not allow this potential disciple to go and bury his father.

The reason seems to be that his father had not yet died! The words "bury my father" did not necessarily refer to the actual burial; it could also refer to the son's living at home until his father's death. Apparently, this man wanted to postpone his obedience to the Lord because of the traditional Jewish obligation to one's father. But the Lord replied that this family responsibility should be left to those who had not heard the Lord's call to service. A study of the remote context would help us to realize that Jesus had nothing against funerals *per se*. He joined funeral mourners on several occasions and worked some of His greatest miracles at funerals (see Luke 7:11–17; John 11:1–45).

The student should become familiar with the ancient customs of the Hebrew people, and with every historical circumstance that might have a bearing on the interpretation of Scripture. While explaining many puzzling aspects of certain passages, the study of the customs and history of the world of the Bible is also an interesting pursuit. Above all, this kind of study can expand the Bible's meaning for our own lives.

For Review

1. In Genesis 19:3 we read that Abraham "baked unleavened bread" for his angelic visitors. Why did he prepare unleavened bread instead of the usual *leavened* bread? Was it because the angels required bread without the "symbol of evil"?

2. When Abraham bought the cave at Machpelah, we are told that he "weighed out...for Ephron... four hundred shekels of silver, currency of the merchant" (Gen. 23:16). Why did he *weigh* the shekels of silver, instead of counting them?

3. According to Genesis 29:23, Laban gave Jacob his daughter Leah instead of Rachel. How is it that Jacob did not realize he had the wrong bride? Recall the rural conditions, the wedding customs, and the feast in order to explain what happened.

9
THE PURPOSE, PLAN, AND LIMITATIONS OF EACH BOOK

The story is told of Benjamin Franklin's being invited by an atheistic society to submit an original story as an entry in a contest. Franklin accepted but submitted the Book of Ruth as though it were his own. When it won first prize, he refused it and explained why. He chided the assembly of atheists, saying that if they had ever read the Bible, which they claimed not to believe, they would have recognized the source of that beautiful piece of literature.

Franklin's use of the story had no connection with the purpose for which it was written; its short-story character was quite incidental to its real message. Ruth was not written primarily to entertain its readership, not to provide good literature, nor even to describe true love in an ancient Hebrew setting. It was most probably written to establish the connection between King David and his Judean ancestors. More incidentally, it may have had the purpose of describing some kindly aspects of Hebrew life in a rebellious period of history.

Casual readers of the Bible are likely to misunderstand the message of any part of Scripture by failing to grasp the reason why it was written. Or they may fail to observe certain literary features that reveal the plan of the book, or to consider that its writer was subject to certain limitations.

The reader should always recognize that each writer had some specific *purpose* in mind for writing; and followed some predetermined *plan;* and due to his position in history and the state of human knowledge at that time, he did not write many things that would have satisfied our modern curiosity.

Purpose

How helpful it would be if Moses had given us more details about creation, the civilization of the Tigris-Euphrates valley, the state of writing, literature, law, and social customs of the period, or other details to show the connection between his account and the various nations of the world! The reason for these omissions is to be found in careful consideration of his purpose for writing that book of beginnings. He was writing a history of God's people, the line of descent that led eventually to the founding of the Hebrew nation. And as he did so, he was recording the earliest history of God's working in the world to bring about the salvation that the human race needed so urgently. Those other details would have made interesting and informative reading, but they were not significant for developing the purpose Moses undoubtedly had in mind.

In the New Testament, the Book of Matthew appears to have been written to set forth Jesus of Nazareth as the promised Messiah and King of Israel. In order to develop that purpose, the writer adopted the plan of presenting those details from the life and ministry of Jesus which would best demonstrate that He was indeed the Messiah and King. The genealogy (see 1:1–16) shows Jesus' connection with Abraham, the father of the nation, with David its ideal king, and with the tribe of Judah, which was to rule over the nation. In this way Matthew attempted to establish Jesus' right to the throne of Israel.

Likewise, Matthew selected a large number of ancient prophecies and showed how Jesus fulfilled them as Messiah and King. Using this plan Matthew carried out his purpose in writing his Gospel.

In the study of each of the four Gospels, the student will notice certain "omissions." Matthew omitted the story of the birth of John the Baptist; perhaps it would have contributed little or nothing to Matthew's purpose. But that same event finds a place in Luke's Gospel, in line with his purpose to tell the complete story for the instruction and benefit of Theophilus: "Having had perfect understanding of all things from the very first . . . that you may know the certainty of those things in which you were instructed" (Luke 1:3–4).

We may observe the same thing with regard to the birth of Jesus. For the purposes of Matthew and Luke the story of Jesus' birth was an essential part of the history, but for Mark and John it was not required. Mark evidently wrote the story in the briefest form for the sake of a readership less accustomed to lengthy theological documents. Some suggest that Mark was writing to Gentiles, presenting Jesus as the Servant of God, and thus the credentials required for a king were unneccessary.

In the case of John's Gospel, there are two possible reasons for the omission of the birth story: his Gospel was supplementary to the other three and intended primarily to include important things they had left out; two of them had already told of Jesus' birth. Or it is possible that because John was presenting Jesus as the eternal Word of God, the story of His birth through Mary was not needed; John referred only to the fact that the Word of God had come to earth: "And the Word became flesh, and dwelt among us, and we beheld His glory, the glory as of the only begotten of the Father, full of grace and truth" (John 1:14).

In the same way we should study any emphasis or omission in each book, in the light of the purpose and plan of the writer, as best we understand them.

Plan

The *plan* is the literary form used by the writer in carrying out his purpose. For example, the Book of the Acts of the Apostles seems to have been written with the purpose of showing the spread of the gospel message from the Jews to the Gentiles and the history of its progress from Jerusalem to Rome. Therefore Luke followed the *plan* of mentioning only those acts of the apostles that were significant in this sense; and he wrote only of the two principal apostles, Peter and Paul, who were the chief exponents of the Jewish and Gentile branches of the faith. Even in their case Luke omitted those acts that did not contribute to the story of the progress of the gospel message from the Jews to the Gentile church, and from the center of Judaism to the capital of the ancient world.

But this is not all: since Acts is primarily a history, largely without commentary, Luke does not interpret the significance of the events he records. It is from the Epistles of Paul that we obtain our interpretation.

The purpose and plan of any book have a close bearing on each other and should be examined together and understood harmoniously.

Limitations

When we speak of the *limitations* of any book of the Bible, we are referring to doctrinal, historic, or scientific matters that the writer did not address because it was not his purpose to do so.

The scientific limitation consists of the basic fact that no book of the Bible was written to discuss science, even though some of its secrets may be found in the Scriptures in an incidental manner. If the Bible refers to a spherical earth (see Is. 40:22), or suggests modern means of travel (see Dan. 12:4), it does so obliquely. It is clear that the writers said such things only in a way incidental to their purpose in writing.

We find many doctrinal limitations in the earlier books of the Bible. We expect to find the gospel in the Old Testament only in terms of promise and prophecy, or in types, symbols, and institutions of the Mosaic Law. Chapter 53 of Isaiah is so remarkable in its direct references to Christ that a Jew hearing it for the first time may feel sure that it belongs in the New Testament rather than the Old. But such direct Old Testament prophecies of Christ are not very common.

Even in the four Gospels, which are selective sketches of the life and ministry of Jesus, there are doctrinal limitations: we do not find the full implications of Christ's death and resurrection in such precise language as in the Book of the Acts and the Epistles. This is due to the fact that the historic aspects of the gospel were accomplished at the very end of the Gospel narrative and the meaning of those events became clear only after Christ's resurrection and Pentecost. With rare exceptions (e.g., Mark 10:45), do we find Jesus making statements comparable to the precise theological language of the gospel found in the later writings. But Jesus Himself warned the disciples that this would be the case, and it was left to John, who wrote last of all, to recall Jesus' words: "These things have I spoken unto you in figurative language; but the time is coming, when I will no longer speak to you in figurative language, but I will tell you plainly about the Father" (John 16:25).

In the Book of the Revelation we are conscious of a very real limitation. As we read, we want to know more of the future but realize that God has not purposed that we should know *now* what needs to be known *only when the time comes*. We feel that God says to us what He said to Daniel: "Go your way . . . the words are closed up and sealed till the time of the end" (Dan. 12:9).

The purpose, plan, and limitations of the books of Scripture are neatly illustrated in the Book of Job, and when we examine these elements in Job carefully we are able to solve some of its problems. The *purpose* of the book seems to be that of showing that the ancient problem of human suffering could not be solved by human wisdom, though Job is one of the most important "wisdom" books. The writer of Job followed the *plan* of recording the speeches of Job's friends, who debated the problem with him and accused him of being a great sinner. In those speeches we observe certain doctrinal *limitations*, especially their ignorance regarding the part played by Satan in the affairs of men.

Nevertheless, the writer understood it and spoke of it in his prologue to the book.

If we should question why Job's friends spoke so much that was true and so much else that was false, the purpose of the book will supply the answer: although they possessed some degree of wisdom, they gave it too much importance in the scheme of things.

The real reason for human suffering is not completely answered in Job; even in the New Testament we do not discover the complete answer. We may say that it exists because it is part of the human situation and was shared by Jesus Christ; or to promote the spiritual development of believers; or to give opportunity to demonstrate faith and love. But we are still subject to certain limitations.

Whenever we offer an interpretation of any part of Scripture, we must be sure that it agrees with the purpose and plan of the book and recognizes the limitations to which the writer was subject.

For Review

1. After reading the Book of Esther, give reasons why the name of God and the subject of prayer are omitted.
2. Read the opening chapters of Proverbs and find the purpose of the book.
3. When we read the history of Israel and the early church in Scripture, why do we not find the history of other nations, such as Egypt, Assyria, Babylonia, Greece, and Rome?
4. Is the history of Israel in the Old Testament a complete history? Explain your answer.

10
THE KEY TO
BOTH TESTAMENTS

When an uninitiated reader of the Bible thoughtfully examines the two Testaments, he may wonder why their tones are so different and how Jesus fits into the Old Testament picture. Without some guidance, it may take a long time to figure how the two Testaments came to be bound as a single book. There is apparently a very great conflict between the Mosaic Law and the Christian gospel. Even those who accept the connection between the two Testaments may have problems distinguishing between the law and the gospel message in Christian living.

A Mexican Christian once asked me whether I fasted as part of my religion. When I answered that, while it is biblical, I did not see fasting as a Christian obligation, he replied, "I fast at least three times a week!"

I asked him for his reason, and he explained it this way: "Jesus said that 'Unless your righteousness exceeds the righteousness of the scribes and Pharisees, you will by no means enter the kingdom of heaven' [Matt. 5:20]. If they fasted twice a week, then I must fast three times a week if my righteousness is to be better than theirs."

As curious as his reasoning may seem, this brother was not alone in his confusion over the matter of righteousness. A large number of Christian Jews of the first century were very rigid in trying to observe the law. Today there are churches that insist on keeping various points of the Mosaic Law. And even the great reformer Martin Luther wrote in his *Commentary on Galatians*, "The law gives all of us trouble."

One reason we have that kind of trouble is the difficulty in distinguishing between the legalistic requirements of the Old Covenant and the gracious promises scattered throughout the Scriptures, particularly in the New Testament.

To understand properly both the old law and the gospel of Christ and to be able to harmonize them in the Person of the Savior, it is absolutely necessary to understand how the two basic covenants differ and what constitutes the message of salvation. This matter belongs more properly to theology than to hermeneutics, but widespread ignorance about the interrelation of the two Testaments requires us to deal with it as an important aspect of biblical interpretation.

Let it be understood that the key to harmonizing the two covenants is Jesus Christ and His gospel. As Saint Augustine put it, "The New is in the Old concealed; the Old is by the New revealed." Christ is the central theme of the Old Testament, even though He does not appear there clearly to the superficial or uninstructed reader.

In the Old Testament, gospel truth was intimated in the ceremonies of the law. In fact, salvation through the mercy and grace of God is the only way salvation is promised anywhere in the Scriptures. The language of the prophets in this regard more often than not served to obscure the gospel rather than to reveal it. However, it is these same prophetic writings that provide numerous gospel promises, clear especially to those who know the gospel of Christ.

The great problem for those who lived under the old legal system was how to be justified before God. Job twice set forth his perplexity: "How can a man be righteous before God?" (Job 9:2; 25:4). Very early God had said through Moses: "You shall therefore keep My statutes and My judgments, which if a man does, he shall live by them" (Lev. 18:5).

The law was a rule of life, designed to guide God's people in obedience and fulfillment. The misunderstanding of such passages as Exodus 19:5; Leviticus 18:5; Deuteronomy 6:25; 27:26; 28:2, coupled with the spiritual blindness of the nation as a whole, allowed the Jews to pursue righteousness in their own strength, as though it were to be obtained by obedience to the law. They tried to save themselves by fulfilling all its requirements (see Rom. 9:31–33; Acts 26:7).

Woven into the fabric of the law was the provision of forgiveness for the sinner. That forgiveness came through the sacrificing of animals, in which their death was required and their blood was sprinkled both on the sinner and the altar. It was true forgiveness even though it came to the sinner through the ceremonial part of the law. Nevertheless, those sacrifices and the whole ceremonial system were designed by the Lord to set forth the gospel plan of forgiveness unto salvation. The blood of those sacrifices was *typical*, or *prophetically symbolic* of the blood of Jesus Christ, "the Lamb of God" (John 1:29,36).

As much as was possible for his place in history,

David understood that God's plan of salvation was wrapped up in the forgiveness of the sinner. In Psalm 32:1-2, he wrote:

Blessed is he whose transgression is forgiven,
Whose sin is covered.
Blessed is the man to whom the Lord does not impute
  iniquity.

The apostle Paul quoted David in the Epistle to the Romans (4:6-8), using this passage as one important Old Testament teaching on the gospel message. We should understand, then, that while the large majority misunderstood the way to be justified under the Old Covenant, some—mostly the prophets—understood it to a limited degree. The truth is that the law itself, with its ceremonies, types, symbols, institutions, prophecies, and promises, testified of the gospel to come, long before it was clearly revealed through the teaching of Christ and the preaching of the apostles.

With the coming of Christ and the gospel, and its fuller explanation in apostolic teaching, we see the fulfillment of the Old Covenant. In Jesus' teaching, He showed how the law was to be observed spiritually, and at the same time He intimated that the Mosaic system would fall into disuse because of its inadequacy (see Matt. 5:17-20).

During the early years of apostolic preaching, the apostles themselves faced difficulty because of the conflict they found between the two religious systems—the Old Covenant (Jewish) and the new (Christian) (see Gal. 2:3-21). Nevertheless, with the transfer of the message of salvation to the Gentile church, evangelical teaching was able to free itself at last from the legalism and intolerance of Judaism.

In our own times the lack of teaching on this subject has allowed many Christians to fall again into a kind of slavery to the old law.

The Bible interpreter and gospel preacher should put forth every effort to understand rightly the imperfection and temporary nature of the law (see Heb. 8:7,13) and to understand the difference between the law interpreted legalistically and the gospel-type promises the ancient believers found in it.

We should note especially the characteristic style of language of the Old Covenant that seemed to suggest salvation was offered as the reward for fulfilling certain works. This was due to the fact that the doctrine of justification by faith was not yet fully revealed; good works, acceptable before God, are the fruit of faith. God did not really promise salvation simply on the basis of obedience to the law; that would have been a genuine contradiction. Christ had to die as God's own sacrifice for sin, and God required faith in the Scriptures including the messianic promises. If it were not so, the Old Testament offers of salvation by the law would involve the use of deceptive language.

Still, a careless interpreter may fall into the error of thinking that there really was, in that Old Testament age, salvation by works, even though he adheres to justification by faith in the present gospel era. The fact is, God was offering salvation to those who obeyed Him with a sincere heart in Old Testament times; for in that obedience, they demonstrated their faith in Him. To recognize Him, to believe in His Word, and to accept His promises of salvation—all of that was involved in the Jews' faithful fulfillment of the law's requirements.

One should note, too, the progressive character of

biblical doctrine. From the beginning to the end of the Bible, we find the development of teachings. The law was the first systematic, elementary revelation of the will of God. The prophets explained the inner spiritual meaning of the law for the Hebrew nation. Christ made it clearer in the Sermon on the Mount, giving new teaching on the subject. At the same time He began to preach the new gospel doctrine in veiled language appropriate to the period before Pentecost. After He rose from the dead and was glorified, He guided the apostles and illuminated their minds by His Spirit. Then they were able to preach with clarity the forgiveness of sin for repentant sinners on the ground of faith in His sacrificial death for them.

In the Epistles we find further explanation of the gospel, together with Christian obligations spelled out, and the newer theme of the work of the Holy Spirit in the believer. There we learn how He teaches, guides, and strengthens believers so that they are enabled to carry out the will of God more effectively.

In the last book of the Bible we discover in some detail the hope of a new world to be governed by the principles of the Christian faith. Likewise, we read more of the propagation of the message of salvation throughout the earth and of the future reign of our Lord, Jesus Christ.

Using this key to the harmonization of the two Testaments, the interpreter will be able to read and understand the biblical message more accurately. In Christ and the gospel we find the only satisfactory explanation of the differences between the Old and New Covenants.

For Review

1. Using what you have learned, attempt to define the gospel message in terms that recognize the earlier expressions of it in the Old Testament.
2. Can you find the gospel message in an elementary form in Genesis 15:6?
3. Do you find room for gospel truth in Exodus 19:5? Explain your answer.

Part II
SPECIAL KEYS TO
UNDERSTANDING
SCRIPTURE

11
FIGURES OF
SPEECH

A better name for Part II of this book would perhaps be "Special Language Forms and Biblical Problems." Basically, we are examining the many varieties of *figurative language,* but for the sake of the traditional terminology, we have kept the usual division of the subject matter.

What *is* figurative language? A quick definition might describe it as any use of words in an unusual sense. *A Complete Guide to Good Writing*[1] says that "a figure of speech is a means of expressing one idea in terms of another which has a real or fancied resemblance to the first." Figurative language is a broader term that includes an even wider variety of literary forms.

Dr. Robert C. McQuilkin, first president of Columbia (S.C.) Bible College, said that on one of his trips he became engaged in conversation with someone sitting next to him. At one point the man asked him, "Isn't it true that the Bible contains much figurative language?"

When McQuilkin replied in the affirmative, the

---

[1]Howard Dunbar, Mildred Marcett, and Frank McCloskey, *A Complete Guide to Good Writing* (New York: D. C. Heath, 1951), p. 234.

man said, "I always knew the Bible had many things in it that are not true."

This gentleman was confusing figurative language with falsehood. The two things have nothing to do with each other. We use figurative language in our daily conversations with no intent to deceive. The biblical writers used it in the same way.

In one sense, all language is figurative. Each word is made up of one or more sounds, which, according to the custom in a given language, are figures or symbols of an idea. The individual written letters are symbols of sounds; and both the written and the spoken word are symbols of the reality they represent. For example, the word "house" represents the object it stands for. The house is the reality; the written and spoken words are figures of the real house. This is why we may say that all language is figurative.

Still, this is not what we mean when we speak of figurative language. In modern cultures the written and spoken words represent the reality, and we speak of this normal use of words as literal language. If we use the word "house" in any other sense, not meaning a literal, real, objective house, we are using it figuratively.

For example, if we speak of "the house of David," we are not talking about a building, but a family or a clan. This is a figurative use of the word. In this case, the figure is a metaphor.

Figures of speech are commonly used to give special effects to language: to introduce a novel idea or to give it force; to communicate a certain shade of meaning; for the sake of beauty; to soften a thought so as to make it acceptable . . . there are many reasons for using figurative language. Its categories are so varied that each particular type has its own name and characteristics. Each must be studied separately.

In this division of the book we will examine the following types of figurative language: figures of speech (covered in this chapter), idioms, types, symbols, parables, allegories, fables, riddles, enigmas, proverbs, poetry, and prophecy. But even those special language forms do not, by any means, exhaust the list.

The Simile

The simile, (pronounced *sih*-mih-lee) is a figure of speech in which any object, action, or relationship is described as being like another dissimilar thing. The simile uses the words *like, as, so, thus,* and *also,* specifically stating the similarity between the two things. This is the simplest figure of speech and the easiest to identify.

See, for example, the similarity specifically declared in this verse:

As snow in summer
   and rain in harvest,
So honor is not fitting for a fool" (Prov. 26:1, italics added).

His meaning is this: Just as snow is not right for summer and as rain should not fall in harvesttime, neither is honor to be given to a fool. Examine the similes in the following texts: Genesis 13:10,16; 15:5; Judges 7:12; Proverbs 26:18–19; Isaiah 1:8.

In some similes the likeness is stated *implicitly*. That is, the similarity between the two things has to be understood by the reader without any specific statement. In Proverbs 26:3 we read: "A whip for the horse,/a

bridle for the donkey,/and a rod for the fool's back."
The writer implies that the three things are equally appropriate.

In Proverbs 25:4–5 we find an *implied simile:*

Take away the dross from silver,
   And it will go to the silversmith for jewelry.
Take away the wicked from before the king,
   And his throne will be established in righteousness.

The student will find an example of a New Testament implied simile in John 12:24–25.

Sometimes the simile is *extended,* and includes several aspects of the similarity. In the Song of Solomon 2:3–5, we have an extended simile:

Like an apple tree among the trees of the woods,
So is my beloved among the sons.
I sat down in his shade with great delight,
And his *fruit was sweet to my taste.*
He brought me to the banqueting house,
And his banner over me was love.
Sustain me with cakes of raisins,
Refresh me with apples,
For I am lovesick.

A parable or an allegory is somewhat like the extended simile. These language forms are treated separately in chapters 16 and 17.

The Metaphor

This figure of speech indicates the likeness between two dissimilar things by *declaring one thing to be the other.* This figure occurs in the words of Jesus in

Matthew 5:14: "You are the light of the world." The words really mean, You are *like* light for the world, perhaps like the light of the sun.

The same figure occurs when the likeness between two dissimilar things is suggested by *words which are proper only to one of them.* In Isaiah 3:15 we read: "What do you mean by *crushing* My people and *grinding* the faces of the poor?" Isaiah uses these words metaphorically, and the whole comparison is called a metaphor.

There is also an *extended metaphor.* In Isaiah 40:7 the prophet says, "Surely the people are grass." But the metaphor is extended in verse 8:

The grass *withers*, the flower *fades*,
But the word of our God stands forever.

In rare cases the writer explains his metaphor, anxious to make sure the reader understands his meaning. In Isaiah 9:14 he says:

Therefore the LORD will cut off head and tail
    from Israel
Palm branch and bulrush in one day.

In using the words "head and tail" he is comparing Israel to a beast. In verse 15 he explains his meaning:

The elder and honorable,
    he is the head;
The prophet who teaches lies,
    he is the tail.

For other examples of the metaphor, see Genesis 15:1; Proverbs 16:22; 25:18; John 10:7; 15:1; Psalm 84:11.

Metonymy

Metonymy (meh-*tah*-nih-mee) is the use of a word in place of another which is intended; the intended word is suggested by the first. When the writer uses *the effect* of an action to suggest its cause, or uses *the symbol or sign* to suggest the reality, he is using metonymy.

In Joel 2:31 the prophet says:

The sun shall be turned into darkness,
And the moon into blood,
Before the coming of the great and terrible day of the LORD.

Here Joel speaks of the effects of God's judgment, which is the cause. But notice that he also uses metaphors: the sun will be "turned into" darkness, that is, it will be darkened; and the moon "into blood," that is, the moon will look like blood.

In 1 John 1:7 the apostle wrote: "If we walk in the light as He is in the light, we have fellowship with one another." Light is a symbol of understanding and righteousness. When he speaks of light in place of the spiritual reality, he is using metonymy.

In Genesis 6:12 and 31:42, the student will find examples of the effect used in place of the cause.

For examples of metonymy that use words suggested by others, see Proverbs 5:15–18 and 23:23. In the first case, the student will also see the use of *euphemism*, discussed later in this chapter.

Synecdoche

This figure of speech (pronounced sih-*neck*-doe-key) occurs when the writer uses *the part for the whole,* or *the whole for the part.* In Psalm 16:9 David says: "My *flesh* also will rest in hope." According to Acts 2:31, he is referring to the resurrection of Christ. Clearly David is not speaking only of his flesh but of his whole body. The word "flesh" does not mean, literally, bones, hair, or fingernails. "Flesh" is a *synecdoche* for the whole body.

There are synecdoches in 1 Corinthians 11:27 and Luke 2:1. But in these same texts, there are also metonymies. These examples show the difficulty we sometimes have in classifying figures of speech.

In Luke 2:1 the evangelist says that Caesar issued an edict to the effect that "all the world should be registered." However, the whole world was not under Caesar Augustus's rule. Luke speaks here only of the part that was really under Caesar's government; that is, the whole for the part. This is the synecdoche. But when he speaks of "all the *world,*" he means the inhabitants of the world. This is the metonymy.

Other examples of synecdoche may be found in Exodus 4:12; Isaiah 32:12; Micah 4:3; and James 1:27.

Irony

Irony is the expression of an idea through its opposite sense, in order to show its absurdity.

Job speaks ironically (12:2) when he says:

No doubt you are the people,
And wisdom will die with you!

His friends were so sure they were right and he was wrong, that Job used this way of calling their attention to the absurdity of their position.

You may examine several ironical expressions in 2 Corinthians 12:11; 1 Kings 18:27; and Job 38:31.

Hyperbole

The word *hyperbole* (pronounced hy-*per*-boe-lee) means in the Greek, "to throw beyond (the target)." As a literary figure, it means the exaggeration of an idea. It should not be thought of as a lie, which, of course, is intended to deceive. The hyperbole exaggerates in an obvious way in order to give emphasis to the thought.

In Deuteronomy 1:28 Moses recalls the words of the spies he had sent to investigate the land. They said that the cities were "great and fortified up to heaven." They wanted to express their conviction that it would be impossible to conquer them. No one understood their words literally, and Moses did not interpret them in a literal sense. Similar language may be found in Numbers 13:32–33.

Examine Genesis 15:5 and ask yourself whether its language is hyperbolic. In Matthew 5:29–30, is there a hyperbole? See also those contained in Proverbs 6:30–31; 23:1–2, and Acts 27:34.

Apostrophe

When words are addressed to a person who is either absent or dead, or to an inanimate thing or abstract idea as though it had life, the expression is called an *apostrophe*.

In 2 Samuel 18:33 David cried out to his dead son: "O my son Absalom—my son, my son Absalom—if only I had died in your place! O Absalom, my son, my son!" David did not imagine that Absalom was able to hear him. But, filled with sorrow, he spoke to his son as though he were present and listening.

In Matthew 23:37–38, the Lord raised His voice in lamentation over the disobedience of the capital city: "O Jerusalem, Jerusalem, the one who kills the prophets and stones those who are sent to her! How often I wanted to gather your children together, as a hen gathers her chicks under her wings, but you were not willing!" In an apostrophe He speaks to the city, that is, to her inhabitants. But they were not present to hear His words.

You will find apostrophes in 1 Corinthians 15:55; Revelation 6:16; Song of Solomon 4:16; Isaiah 1:2; 52:9. Think carefully about Mark 4:39. Does it contain an apostrophe?

Personification

This figure of speech exists when personal characteristics are attributed to animals, plants, or inanimate objects. In passing only, we mention that it is sometimes called *prosopopoeia.*

In Isaiah 55:12 the prophhct says:

The mountains and the hills
Shall break forth into singing before you,
And all the trees of the field shall clap their hand.

Unless there were some grotesque, unnecessary miracle, inanimate things could never sing or clap hands. A careful reading of the context shows that the prophet refers to the miracle that happens in the believers' hearts as a result of the work of the Savior. This is clear from the first part of the verse, which declares:

For you shall go out with joy,
And be led out with peace.

The words that follow, saying that the mountains and
hills will sing, should be understood as the poetic
complement of the former part of the verse, in which
the joy of the redeemed is personified in nature.

In Proverbs 1:20–23 wisdom is personified. Solomon wrote:

Wisdom calls aloud outside;
She raises her voice in the open squares.

Some readers understand verses 24–33 as the voice of
God, but according to the statement in verse 20, the
whole passage is properly classified as a personification of wisdom. Again in Proverbs 8:1–31 the same
figure appears.

Other examples may be found in Isaiah 14:8;
35:1–2; 44:23. In this latter text the student will notice
the presence of an apostrophe as well.

Euphemism

Euphemism (*yu*-feh-mism) is the substitution of
acceptable words for others that may offend the hearers or readers. Instead of saying that a person urinates
or has a bowel movement or describing the act with
crude slang phrases, the speaker may say that he or
she "used the toilet," "went to the bathroom," "ex-
cused himself," or "powdered her nose." These are
modern euphemisms.

In Deuteronomy 23:13 we read the words: "When
you sit down outside" to mean "defecate." The words
are the same in the original Hebrew, indicating a similar feeling for delicacy in speech in Old Testament
times.

In 1 Kings 18:27 Elijah taunts the Baal-worshipers, saying that their god "is gone aside" according to the American Standard Version; in the Good News Bible we find "relieving himself." The sense of this euphemism is very clear in the latter translation.

The sexual act, cohabitation, is expressed in a number of ways in the Scriptures. In Genesis 49:4 Jacob says to his son Reuben, "You went up to your father's bed; Then you defiled it—He went up to my couch." These are ways of referring to his sexual misconduct. In the Good News Bible the reference is even clearer: "You slept with my concubine and dishonored your father's bed." Even so, *sleeping with* and *dishonoring* are other euphemisms.

In Genesis 4:1, we read that "Adam *knew* Eve his wife." But the same word is used in 19:5 with reference to a homosexual act. In Genesis 39:7 Potiphar's wife says to Joseph, "Lie with me." As acceptable as these euphemisms are in English, none falls so pleasantly on the ear as those found in Proverbs 5:18–19: "*Rejoice* with the wife of your youth. . . . Let her *breasts satisfy* you at all times;/And always be *enraptured* with her love."

Leviticus 18:6–20 uses several different expressions in referring to intercourse, the most frequent term being "uncover the nakedness." In Mark 7:19, Jesus refers to emptying the bowels as to what "is eliminated." And Peter, avoiding the reference to Judas's condemnation in hell, says that he went "to his own place" (Acts 1:25).

Paradox

When apparently contradictory truths are expressed in immediate connection with each other, such as in the same verse or sentence, that seeming contradiction is called a paradox. There are many paradoxes in Jesus' teaching.

For example, the high priest demanded of Jesus in Mark 14:61–62: "Are you the Christ, the Son of the Blessed?" Jesus replied: "I am. And you will see the Son of Man sitting at the right hand of the Power, and coming with the clouds of heaven." To His hearers, being the Son of God and the Son of Man at the same time was contradictory. It was, of course, a paradox.

In the Beatitudes (Matthew 5) there are several paradoxes. In verse 4 Jesus teaches: "Blessed are those who mourn," even though blessedness (happiness) is not usually associated with mourning. In verse 5, He says: "Blessed are the meek,/For they shall inherit the earth." In human society the meek are almost never the ones who receive such power. And in verses 10–12, those who are persecuted are said to possess the kingdom of God and are told to rejoice. All of these apparently contradictory teachings are paradoxes.

Many paradoxes may also be classified as enigmas. These will be studied in Chapter 17.

Play on Words

This figure of speech is found in a number of places in the Bible. It links two similar-sounding words together, to emphasize a point. Solomon used it in the Song of Solomon, and Paul did so in several of his letters.

In the Song of Solomon 1:3, the bride says of the king: "Your name is ointment poured forth." The play on words appears only in the Hebrew text. The word "name" is *shem*, and the word "ointment" is *shemen*. The play on words is more easily identified if we read "Thy *shem* is *shemen* poured forth."

The same play on words is found in Ecclesiastes 7:1, where we read: "A good name (*shem*) is better than precious ointment (*shemen*)."

In his letter to Philemon, Paul asked that Onesimus be set free from bondage to his master. Onesimus's name means "profitable." But since he had run away from Philemon, he did not turn out to be as profitable as his name suggested. But now, through the ministry of Paul and the change in Onesimus's life, his name took on meaning. In verse 11 Paul wrote concerning Onesimus, "who once was *unprofitable* to you, but now is *profitable* to you and to me." The play on words calls attention to the miraculous change that God had produced in him.

Each of the above examples depends for its meaning on the original texts in Hebrew and Greek. But there are others whose meaning comes through clearly in English.

In Philippians 3:2-3, Paul warned his readers to "beware of the *mutilation!* For we are the *circumcision*, who worship God in the Spirit." The *mutilation* refers, of course, to the Jews who practiced circumcision on their male children as required by the Mosaic Law. It was intended to be a constant reminder of their separation from the way of the flesh unto God. But Paul here claims this spiritual characteristic of separation from the way of the flesh for Christian believers and calls the Jews "the concision" (KJV), or "the cutters of the flesh." The New International Version uses the expression "those mutilators of the flesh," while the Good News Bible says: "those men who insist on *cut-*

ting the body." By using this term in a play on words, Paul speaks in a derogatory manner of their false emphasis.

But Paul uses the same word with genuine anger in Galatians 5:11–12. Speaking of those who taught the necessity of being circumcised, he says: "I could wish that those who trouble you would even cut themselves off," or "mutilate themselves" (ASV). Note how the translators of the American Standard Version preferred the euphemism "go beyond circumcision" rather than the more brutal meaning. The Good News Bible puts is very bluntly: "let them go on and castrate themselves." In both these latter texts, the play on words comes through in English very clearly.

For Review

Look up the texts cited at the end of each discussion of the various figures of speech and identify the figure of speech used in each text.

12
HEBREW IDIOMS

Visiting in Pottstown, Pennsylvania, part of Pennsylvania Dutch country, a salesman entered the office of a local businessman. When the salesman admired a piece of calendar art on the wall, the businessman startled him by ordering: "Hang it off!" The secretary took the art down and gave it to her employer, who then offered it as a gift to the salesman.

Except for having heard and seen what happened, the salesman would not have understood the meaning of the expression "Hang it off!" The Pennsylvania Dutchman had used an idiom common only among his people.

Among Americans as a whole, expressions like the following are easily understood: hit the hay, trip the light fantastic, cut corners, touch base, throw a curve, be a Monday-morning quarterback, burn the midnight oil. And in every culture and subculture members of the group use a wide variety of idioms understood only by other members of the group; outsiders need an explanation because the words do not have an obvious, literal sense.

Webster's New Collegiate Dictionary defines the idiom as "an expression in the usage of a language that is peculiar to itself either grammatically or in having a meaning that cannot be derived from the conjoined meanings of its elements." In simpler terms, it is an expression not easily understood, or meant in a sense different from its literal meaning.

Hebrew idioms differ from the usual figures of speech in that the latter are often understood even though the reader may have never seen or heard them before. Idioms, however, are understandable only to those who speak the language or to those who have studied the language and customs of the people.

In the older translations of the Bible, the idioms of the Old Testament were often translated literally, resulting in somewhat meaningless phrases. Modern translators have done better in this regard, often substituting equivalent English-language idioms. In any case, when we read the Bible, especially the older versions, we may find idioms that have not been adequately rendered in translation.

We should keep in mind that Hebrew idioms are not found exclusively in the Old Testament. In spite of the fact that the New Testament was written in Greek, some Hebrew idioms are found there too. The New Testament was written mostly by Jews whose Greek had been influenced by the Hebrew language. But undoubtedly the principal way in which Hebrew idioms worked their way into the New Testament was through the Greek translation of the Old Testament, the *Septuagint.* And since the larger part of the early Christian community was Jewish, the language of the early church was affected.

The Hebrew idioms we will study in this chapter are the following:

The absolute for the relative

The relative for the absolute

The idiom of sonship
Several idioms of time
Anthropomorphism
Ellipsis

The Absolute for the Relative

The full expression for this kind of idiom should be "Absolute language used in place of relative language," but the technical name is "the absolute for the relative."

Absolute language is that which speaks positively without allowing for doubt or error; it uses superlatives and absolutes. When words such as *good, bad, always, never, yes,* and *no* are used, this is absolute language. We also have it in various instructions or prohibitions that allow no room for deviation.

Relative language is the kind that expresses some type of comparison or preference. This is found in words such as *better, worse, more, less, larger,* and *smaller*—whatever expresses comparison.

The idiom known as "the absolute for the relative" means the use of absolute language where the *sense intended is only relative.*

T. Norton Sterrett in his book on interpretation suggests a good way to recognize this type of idiom. "First, consider it as a literal statement. Does it make sense? If it does not, then consider it as an idiom. Study it in its context, and you will see some confirmation that you have the right meaning."[1]

You may notice the similarity between this idiom and the figure of speech called hyperbole, which is common in many languages. However, this idiom is

---

[1]T. Norton Sterrett, *How to Understand Your Bible* (Downers Grove, Ill.: Inter-Varsity, 1974), p. 127.

especially Hebrew. One of the main differences is the kind of exaggeration. The hyperbole always exaggerates in an obvious way, while the exaggeration in the absolute for the relative is not always so evident.

A clear example of the use of absolute language with the relative sense is found in Proverbs 8:10:

Receive my instruction, and *not* silver;
And knowledge *rather than* choice gold.

The writer is saying that one should give preference to his instruction over precious metals. This sense is clear when we look at the last part of the verse: "[My instruction is to be chosen] *rather than* choice gold." Recognizing the idiom informs us that the writer is not prohibiting us from receiving silver as the first part of the verse says. When we compare the teaching of the rest of the Bible, we realize that we are not prohibited from receiving silver or gold in every case. Work is properly compensated with money.

The expression, "Receive my instruction and not silver," is the use of absolute language with the relative sense. There are several possible reasons why the writer did not say immediately what he said later, "Receive my instruction rather than silver." He may have wanted to vary his words to avoid the monotony of repeating the same expression, or he may have thought the expressions were equivalent. Again, he may have written the second line to clarify the first. We know, too, that the practice of repeating the same thought in slightly different words is a characteristic of Hebrew poetry, which we will study in Chapter 18.

We find this kind of idiom again in Luke 14:12: "When you give a dinner or a supper, *do not ask your friends, your brothers, your relatives, nor your rich neighbors*, lest they also invite you back, and you be repaid."

Was the Lord saying that we should never invite friends, brothers, relatives, or rich neighbors to eat with us? Of course not, except with regard to a heavenly reward (see v. 14). He teaches that we should be concerned about the poor and unfortunate as a Christian duty. We are not to think of having dinners only with our own interests in mind.

From this we may see that Jesus has not absolutely forbidden us to invite those who might be able to return the favor. Even though the instruction is given in absolute terms, the point is relative. Those who humble themselves to invite the poor are rewarded at the resurrection.

There is another idiom similar to the absolute for the relative, called the *idiom of hatred*. In Genesis 29:31 we read: "And Jehovah saw that Leah was *hated*" (ASV). Nevertheless, the context shows that the word "hated" is not used with its normal force. Verse 30 says merely that Jacob "loved also Rachel more than Leah." To say that he hated her, means only that he loved her with less intensity than he loved Rachel, her sister. The Good News Bible changes the expression in verse 31 from "hated" to "loved less," and the New King James Version reads "unloved." This is the proper sense.

In Luke 14:26 we read what sounds like a very strange sentiment: "If anyone comes to Me and *does not hate* his father and mother, wife and children, brothers and sisters, yes, and his own life also, he cannot be My disciple." Here again, the word "hate" is used in the sense of "loved less." Jesus used this absolute language in place of weaker, relative words. He intended to show that love for Him must be supreme, because He is over all. Other loves must appear as hate in comparison to it.

Examine the following texts and answer the questions to distinguish the relative meaning in each text.

Deuteronomy 5:2–3. Did God not make a covenant with "the fathers"?

Matthew 9:13. Did God not want sacrifices? Compare Hosea 6:6.

Matthew 19:23–26. Is it possible for the rich to be saved?

John 12:25. Was Jesus saying that we ought to commit suicide?

1 Peter 3:3–4. Is it wrong to use beauty aids?

The Relative for the Absolute

This idiom is the reverse of the former and consists of the use of relative language when the sense is absolute. It is the use of weak language to express what is strong, rich, great, or infinite.

In Luke 18:14 we read that "this man [the publican] went down to his house justified *rather than* the other." If we were to take this expression literally, we might think that the Pharisee, too, was justified, even though it was not as easy as it was in the case of the publican, who was to be preferred over him in this matter. But the parable teaches that the publican was not justified at all. In spite of the words "rather than," we know that the teaching of the parable is absolute.

Study the following texts and answer the questions to determine the absolute meaning.

Matthew 5:20. By how much must our righteousness exceed that of the scribes and Pharisees? Or, in what way must it exceed that of those men?

Matthew 10:31. How much more than the sparrows are we worth?

Hebrews 9:23. How much better is the blood of Christ than that of the animal sacrifices?

The Idiom of Sonship (or Filiation)

Frequently we find such expressions as "the son of [someone or something]." When the purpose of this phrase is to indicate one of several kinds of relationship, it is classified as the idiom of sonship. The relationships included may be physical, moral, or spiritual, but *not literal.*

Normally, the words "son of someone" are to be understood literally. When Jesus said to Peter, "Simon, son of Jonah" (John 21:15), he spoke *literally.* This is not the idiom of sonship.

But in Acts 3:25 Peter was reported as saying: "You are the sons of the prophets." They were not literally sons of the prophets, because all except John the Baptist had died hundreds of years earlier. The clear meaning is that they were their *descendants,* physically. And because they were not literal sons of the prophets, this expression is the idiom of sonship in the physical sense.

In Ephesians 5:8 the apostle wrote: "Walk as children of light." He was referring to those who had the light of God and the gospel living in them. The relationship between the converted individual and the light of heaven is expressed by means of the idiom of sonship.

Examine the following texts and write out the meaning of each one: Matthew 5:45; Luke 7:35; 10:6; Ephesians 2:3; 5:6.

Idioms of Time

Eternity. The Hebrews used the words *eternity, eternal, forever, perpetual, everlasting,* and similar expressions in two ways: literally and temporally and sometimes in a double sense.

The following texts illustrate their literal usage.

Lest he put out his hand and take also of the tree of life, and eat, and live *forever* (Gen. 3:22).

This is My name *forever,* and this is My memorial *to all generations* (Ex. 3:15).

The *eternal* God is your refuge, and underneath are the *everlasting* arms (Deut. 33:27).

The following passages illustrate the use of such expressions in a limited, *temporal* sense:

I will make you an *eternal* excellence. A joy of *many generations* (Is. 60:15).

Since the prophet was speaking of Israel as a nation, he uses these expressions in a temporal sense; neither Israel as a nation nor the human race as a whole would last forever. The meaning is limited to the existence of human beings on earth.

So this day shall be to you a memorial; and you shall keep it as a feast to the LORD *throughout your generations.* You shall keep it as a feast by an *everlasting* ordinance (Ex. 12:14).

That historic day could be kept only as long as the

Mosaic Law was in force. With the coming of Christ, this and other ceremonies ordered by the law, fell into disuse. The word *forever* clearly has a limited meaning.

In some prophetic texts these words are used in both ways: in a limited way with regard to the immediate future, and literally whenever they refer to Christ and His kingdom.

In 2 Samuel 7:13 we read: "He [Solomon] shall build a house for My name, and I will establish the throne of his kingdom *forever*." Insofar as the words refer to Solomon, the sense must be limited, because the royal dynasty ended with the deportation of Israel to Babylon. But with regard to Christ, who came into the world through the royal line, His throne and kingdom are forever. In this latter sense the language is literal. One single text is used in a double sense.

The student may examine the following texts to determine in what sense the expression of eternity is used: Leviticus 25:45–46; Genesis 17:13; Numbers 25:13; Isaiah 32:14–15; Revelation 1:18; Mark 9:44 (KJV).

Parts of days. The Hebrews regarded the day as composed of evening and morning (Gen. 1:5). Any part of the twenty-four-hour period was counted legally as a whole day. For this reason the expression "on the third day" meant the same as "after three days." In some modern cultures, notably the Spanish-speaking countries, the same custom is still in use.

In the following verses, see examples of this idiom: "Depart for *three days*, then come back to me" (1 Kin. 12:5). Then in verse 12 we read: "So Jeroboam and all the people came to Rehoboam *the third day, as the king directed, saying, Come back to me the third day."* "So he put them all together in prison three days" (Gen. 42:17). Then verse 18 reads: "Then Joseph said to them *the third day,* Do this and live."

In the case of Jesus' resurrection, the same idiom is used. The following texts state that Jesus would stay in the tomb for *three days:* Matthew 12:40; Mark 8:31; John 2:19. Nevertheless, other texts say that He would rise *on the third day:* Luke 24:46; Acts 10:40; 1 Corinthians 15:4; and others. Note that when the Jews went before Pilate they used the two expressions interchangeably (Matt. 27:63–64).

Anthropomorphism

This word is made up of two Greek words: *anthrō̄pos,* man, and *morphēs,* form. Together they mean "in human form."

This idiom consists of speaking of God in words that are properly used only of human beings. God is a Spirit and, as such, has no body nor bodily members. And because He is an infinite Being, He is not subject to human limitations. When speaking of Him as though He were a man, the writers use the idiom of anthropomorphism.

Reasons for its use should be evident. In order to speak of God's actions in any way, we use words drawn from human experience. It is most natural, if not necessary, to say God *hears* our prayers, *sees* our actions, *comes* to help us, *forgets* our sins, or *hides* His face from sinners. But all of these expressions describe the way human beings do things; we can hardly speak of God in any other way. See the following examples:

Exodus 8:19 speaks of "the finger of God."

Exodus 33:11 says that Moses spoke to God "face to face."

Genesis 6:7 states that God was sorry for having made man, even though Numbers 23:19 says that "God is not a man . . . that He should repent."

Jeremiah 7:13 says of God that He *rises up early* and *speaks.*

Psalm 18:11 speaks of darkness as God's *secret place; His canopy around Him was dark waters.* And the apostle Paul speaks of Him as *dwelling in the light* (1 Tim. 6:16).

We should avoid criticizing the writers of Scripture when they speak of God in human terms. They are communicating in the most natural and normal way and undoubtedly giving us a clearer idea of God.

Ellipsis

When any text expresses a thought without using all the words required by the rules of modern grammar, we call that usage an *ellipsis.* In such cases the reader must add certain words to make the expression read the way it should for the eyes and ears of English-speaking people. Sometimes it is necessary to change the form of a sentence as it stands in the original language, especially if the writer has changed his subject suddenly without indicating the connection between his thoughts. From the viewpoint of English grammar, this may appear as a defect in the original writing, but we do not know all the rules by which biblical writers governed their writing. What we know of ancient grammar does not tell us enough to make critical judgments of those who wrote the books of the Bible. In any case, apparent defects in grammatical structure should be regarded as the idiom of ellipsis.

In Acts 18:6 Paul wrote, "Your blood be upon your

own heads; I *am* clean." The italics here indicate that the word *am* is not in the original; the expression "I, clean" is elliptical. The New International Version augments the English translation considerably, saying, "I am clear of my responsibility."

In Romans 8:3 Paul wrote: "For what the law could not do, in that it was weak through the flesh, God, sending his own Son in the likeness of sinful flesh, and for sin, condemned sin in the flesh" (KJV). The unwieldy phraseology obscures the fact that the sentence is not grammatically complete as it stands. In order to give a complete thought, the New King James Version, New International Version, and Good News Bible translators have inserted the verb "did," that is, "what the law could not do . . . God *did* by sending His own Son."

In some cases the translators have found it necessary to add several words in the translation. These are printed in italics in the New King James Version and in the American Standard Version, while the Good News Bible and New International Version have adjusted the translations without comment. None of the latter versions uses italics to complete any ellipses. The italics in the two passages below indicate words added for clarity by the New King James Version translators.

I fed you with milk and not with solid food; for until now you were not able *to receive it*, and even now you are still not able (1 Cor. 3:2).

Therefore He who supplies the Spirit to you and works miracles among you, *does He do it* by the works of the law, or by the hearing of faith? (Gal. 3:5).

For Review

Review the questions at the end of the discussions on:

1. the absolute for the relative
2. the relative for the absolute
3. the idiom of sonship
4. the idioms of time.

13
TYPES

The New Testament writings use another kind of figurative language called the *type*. Certain persons, places, objects, events, and institutions of Old Testament times were prepared by the Lord to represent some future spiritual reality. They were figures or types of those realities.

The study of types is a matter of controversy. Some teachers of biblical interpretation would like to see the study of types eliminated completely. Still, the word *type* is biblical, and numerous parts of the New Testament depend on it for their proper interpretation.

The Greek word *tupos* is behind our English word *type*, though *tupos* is usually translated as *figure*. This is a bit confusing for the Bible student, because *figure* also translates *antitupos* (antitype) and *parabolē* (parable). In order to distinguish properly between the terms, this literary figure will be called a type in this study.

We will note first of all, that the type is a figure of a future spiritual reality, occurring as such by inspiration. All types are prophetic; they are not merely apt illustrations. Consequently, the only way to be sure that an Old Testament illustration is really a type is to be able to point to some New Testament confirmation of it.

But there is a problem with this: if a type must be validated on the basis of New Testament references to it as such, we will reject some that are too clear to be eliminated. More will be said on this subject later. Meanwhile, such potential types may be regarded as *probable* or *possible* types. Others, whose character appears to be forced, should be ignored or left in a doubtful category.

A second characteristic of the type is that it represented a spiritual reality whose fullness would be revealed only after the coming of Christ. However, those persons, places, events, objects, and institutions, now called types, contained in themselves notable spiritual values, apart from later fulfillment.

If the type prefigures a spiritual reality, the *antitype* is the fulfillment of it. In ancient times, the Messiah was the great future spiritual reality. In the New Testament He is the great Antitype that corresponds to the Old Testament originals.

Even though types have varied forms, the greater part of them are fulfilled in Christ. Sometimes they were certain *persons* of biblical history. Others were certain *offices* provided for in the Mosaic Law. In some cases they were physical *objects*, or significant *places*, historical *events*, or *institutions* of the Hebrew religious system. Whenever the New Testament indicates that any one of these represents Christ or some reality of His spiritual kingdom, we may be sure that it is a true type.

Among the typical *persons* are Adam (see Rom. 5:14); Abraham and Isaac (see Heb. 11:17–19); Moses (see Deut. 18:18; John 1:21, 45; Acts 7:37); Joshua (see

Josh. 1:15; Heb. 4:8); Melchizedek (see Ps. 110:4; Heb. 6:20–7:25); David (see Is. 55:3; Acts 2:25–32); Solomon (see 2 Sam. 7:12–16; Matt. 12:42); Jonah (see Matt. 12:40), and others.

The typical *offices* are those of prophet (Deut. 18:15–18; John 4:19,44; Acts 3:22–26); priest (Ps. 110:4; Heb. 5:1–10); king (Jer. 23:5–6; Zech. 9:9; John 1:49; Matt. 21:1–11); liberator (Is. 61:1; Luke 4: 18–19) and judge (Is. 11:3–4; 2 Tim. 4:1).

The following historical *events* are types: the offering of one of Abel's flock; the offering of Isaac and the substitution of the ram; the passing over of Israel's firstborn in Egypt; the crossing of the Red Sea; the entrance into the land of Canaan, and others which the student will be able to identify.

Certain physical *objects* were types: Noah's ark; the ram that was substituted for Isaac; the passover lamb; the rock that was struck in the desert; the manna; the bronze serpent; Jacob's ladder; the ark of the covenant; the veil of the temple; the tabernacle and all of its furniture.

Typical *places* include the Jordan River; the land of Canaan; Egypt; the desert of Sinai; Jerusalem; Babylon; Tyre and Sidon.

The typical *institutions* of the Law are: the annual passover feast; all the feasts established by the law; the priesthood; all the sacrifices of the law; the temple; circumcision; the cities of refuge; the various kinds of sabbath, and others.

After identifying any type, you may proceed to interpret it. The following procedure should be helpful:

1. Read everything the Bible says about the fulfillment of the specific type.

2. Make a list of the details mentioned in the Old

Testament concerning the type. Afterwards, make a second list opposite the first, showing in which points and in what way the details of the type are fulfilled in the antitype.

3. Note well the significance of the historical event in the life of those who experienced it. This will show what value the event had for those who lived through it. Try to apply the same question to people, places, objects, offices, and institutions.

4. Identify the principal message of the type by examining the New Testament references to it.

The case of the serpent in the wilderness will serve as an example of this procedure. The first step will be to identify the case as a type, according to some New Testament reference. This is found in John 3:14-15. "And as Moses lifted up the serpent in the wilderness, even so must the Son of Man be lifted up, that whoever believes in him should not perish but have eternal life." (This is the only New Testament text that refers to the event.) Next we will make parallel lists indicating how the details of the type are fulfilled.

Type (Numbers 21:4-9)	Antitype (John 3:14-15)
1. The people sinned against God and Moses.	1. All have sinned (Rom. 3:23).
2. The serpents bit the people and many died.	2. Sin passed to all men (Rom. 5:12) and all died spiritually.
3. The people confessed their sin and asked forgiveness.	3. All people need to repent (Mark 1:15).
4. Moses prayed for the people.	4. Christ prays for us (Heb. 7:25).
5. God ordered a serpent made of bronze.	5. God made Christ to be sin for us (2 Cor. 5:21).
6. God promised (physical) life to those who looked toward the serpent.	6. All who believe in Him will have eternal life (John 3:15).

7. Moses obeyed, lifting up the serpent on a staff.

7. It was necessary for Christ to be lifted up (John 3:14).

8. Everyone who looked to the serpent was saved from death.

8. All who believe today in Jesus Christ are saved (John 3:15–16).

In points 6, 7, and 8 we can identify the principal message of the type, as indicated in the fourth step of the procedure. The other points of the history agree with this central message and support it. In teaching this typical event, all of the above points may be made profitably without forcing or twisting the message.

Returning to step number three, we ask: What was the value of the historical event for those who lived through it? First, we should admit that it is unlikely that any of those who witnessed this event, including Moses, understood it as a prophetic type. Those who were dying from the serpents' bites received the promise with gratitude because they were to be saved from death by looking at the bronze serpent. That was God's provision for their physical healing in the midst of a deadly situation. But when they reflected on it later, the bronze serpent undoubtedly became a vivid reminder of their sin, because God had sent the "fiery" serpents as punishment when they murmured against Him. It is also possible that the bronze became for them a symbol of divine judgment on sin.

In a word, the bronze serpent lifted up in the sight of all the people was God's call to recognize that He had judged their sin and that they were to repent of it. His promise was a most gracious offer of life.

A similar procedure may be used to teach the message of any type.

A word of warning: it is neither necessary nor proper to assign typical or allegorical meanings to every event of Bible history. The events of biblical history contain profitable lessons for us today, whether in a positive or a negative sense. But there is no need to allegorize them or search for subtle typical meanings which the Holy Spirit has not clearly indicated.

Having said the above, it should be recognized that there are undoubtedly typical persons and events not mentioned in the New Testament. The problem is how to recognize them without straining the facts. Mickelsen suggests three "rigorous guide rules" to help in identifying these types.[1] In abbreviated form the rules are as follows:

- A potential type must show a similarity to the antitype in some basic *quality* or *element*.
- The basic *quality* or *element* should exhibit God's purpose in the historical context of the *type* and also God's purpose in the historical context of the *antitype*.
- That which is taught by typological correspondence must also be taught by direct assertion.

If these rules are applied to the case of the patriarch Joseph, we find that he did indeed show a similarity to Christ when he generously forgave his brothers, who regarded him as their enemy. Of Jesus this is obviously true. All His ministry is characterized in both His teaching and actions by grace and forgiveness toward sinners. He prayed: "Father, forgive them, for they do not know what they do" (Luke 23:34). We also see Him promising the repentant thief on the cross a place with Him in paradise (Luke 23:43).

In the historical context, Joseph recognized and spe-

---

[1]Mickelsen, *Interpreting the Bible*, p. 263.

cifically stated God's purpose in sending him to Egypt "to save your lives" (Gen. 45:7). And in the case of both type and antitype, the fact and example of forgiveness and the resulting salvation is specifically stated (Gen. 50:19–21; Eph. 1:7; Tit. 2:11–15).

A study of Joseph's life will also reveal a number of important points of correspondence between his life and that of Jesus. These would include Joseph's righteous and exemplary conduct, the undeserved enmity of his brothers and the wife of Potiphar, his prophetic ministry, the unparalleled authority he was given as vice-regent of Egypt, and the salvation resulting from his ministry, both for the Hebrews and for many Egyptians.

Mickelsen's rules should help settle the question of the typical value of many Old Testament persons and events not mentioned in the New Testament as types.

For Review

1. Locate and read the New Testament references that verify the types mentioned in this chapter.
2. Examine the information available on the following persons and tell why they should or should not be regarded as types of Christ: Jacob, Caleb, Samuel, Elijah, Jeremiah, Daniel, and Hosea.

14
SYMBOLS

On the afternoon of January 20, 1981, the American people received word that the fifty-two hostages held in Iran were on their way to freedom. When those released captives reached the United States, they were greeted with an unprecedented outpouring of joy by the entire nation. Yellow ribbons were tied to any available tree, signpost, or building, symbolizing welcome after 444 days of confinement. One commentator said, "I didn't know there was that much yellow ribbon in all the world!"

The symbolism of the yellow ribbon was drawn from a popular song "Tie a Yellow Ribbon 'Round the Old Oak Tree."

Curiously, yellow had taken on a new meaning for the public. Traditionally it had been a symbol of cowardice; but in 1981, it meant "Welcome home, Hostages!" The change of meaning illustrates one of the notable characteristics of symbols: their meanings may change in different contexts.

A symbol may be defined as any real, visible thing that represents something invisible. The invisible thing may be an idea, a quality, or a spiritual reality, according to the association between the two.

Symbols may be objects, substances, colors, or numbers, and their meanings depend on the intention of the one who uses them. As Mickelsen insists, the author's meaning must be determined through inductive study, that is, through the careful examination of each individual case.[1] In the Bible, it is necessary to examine a symbol's many uses in different contexts before deciding whether it has a fixed value.

Many symbols have come to have a fixed significance, even though it is contrary to their nature as symbols to have any permanent meaning. In our own culture, red and green, light and darkness, gold and silver, almost always represent fixed ideas. But it is also common to find symbols whose meanings are not only varied but completely contrary in other contexts. This is particularly true in the Bible.

For example, the lion may symbolize strength or royalty, and the two ideas do not contradict one another. The lion may also represent protection; or it may stand for that which is frightening and evil. In Revelation 5:5 Christ is called "the Lion of the tribe of Judah." But in 1 Peter 5:8 the devil is compared to a lion: "your adversary the devil walks about like a roaring lion." Again, in Daniel 7:4 the lion symbolizes the first world kingdom under Nebuchadnezzar.

Water symbolizes many things in the Bible. In 2 Chronicles 18:26 it represents anguish. But in John 2 it is understood as the symbol of what is common or usual in life. In Ephesians 5:26 water represents the preached Word of God: "sanctify and cleanse it with the washing of water by the word." In John 7:38–39 water symbolizes the Spirit of God. In Matthew 27:24

---

[1]Mickelsen, *Interpreting the Bible*, pp. 272, 278.

it stands for washing or cleansing. In Jonah 2:5–6 water symbolizes the grave. In Revelation 22:1 it represents eternal life.

We usually think of the lamb as a symbol of Jesus crucified for sin; in John 1:29 He is the "Lamb of God." But the lamb also represents the child or the recent convert (see John 21:15).

Most frequently, leaven is a symbol of evil, hypocrisy, or corruption (see 1 Cor. 5:7), but not always. In Matthew 13:33 the extension of God's kingdom is compared to the action of leaven in a mass of dough. In itself, leaven is not an evil thing, because it was acceptable to God in the offering of the firstfruits (see Lev. 2:11–12). In this case, leaven cannot represent evil, but instead joy and abundance in the life of the believer.

In certain cases birds represent Satan, as in Matthew 13:4,19. In Revelation 18:2 they represent abominations. But in Psalm 124:7 they symbolize the trusting soul. In Song of Solomon 2:12 they represent springtime, and in Isaiah 31:5, protection. In Isaiah 40:31 they represent "those who wait on the LORD", that is, His faithful and patient servants.

Oil is nearly always understood as a symbol of the Holy Spirit. This symbolism is based on the use of oil in the anointing of the Hebrew kings. In the New Testament (1 John 2:20) the gift of the Holy Spirit is called an "anointing," a metonymy referring to the oil of the Old Testament ceremonies. In other texts oil is used as a symbol of medicine (see Is. 1:6; James 5:14). It is used also to represent gladness (see Heb. 1:9; Is. 61:3), and in Revelation 6:6 and Joel 2:24, it represents food.

In interpreting symbols, one must always keep in

mind that their meaning depends on some likeness between them and the things they represent. For this reason the likeness is usually *simple, not multiple.* The symbol and the thing symbolized are alike in a single point, not several, so the meaning of the symbol should be limited to whatever is most evident. This likeness is what gives the symbol its true value.

When, for example, water represents the Word of God, it is because both things *cleanse*; not because they are clear, refreshing, inexpensive, or healthful. When oil symbolizes the Holy Spirit, it is because the individual is anointed with both. Oil is not symbolic of the Spirit because it gives light when it burns, nor because it is used to soften the scab on a wound, nor because it is extracted from the fruit only when it is pressed. Searching for several points of similarity is faulty handling of the symbol.

Symbols versus Types

There is a close relationship between types and symbols: both are visible signs of something invisible. But they differ in the following points:

- The type is complex, being composed of various significant details, while the symbol represents a single point of likeness.
- The type is always fulfilled at a specific time, while the symbol is not subject to the limitations of time.
- The type is found only in the Bible, while symbols are common to all language and literature.

Normally, types contain symbols; but these symbols only help to present the complex picture contained in the type. In themselves, the symbols do not have special prophetic significance.

For example, the type found in the lifting up of the serpent in the wilderness contains several symbols: the *serpent* represents sin; while the *brass* or *bronze* represents judgment. Together, the two symbols represent God's judgment on sin. The whole event is called a type and is prophetic of the death of Christ and of the gospel. But the symbols of serpent and brass represent realities that are timeless, apart from their presence in the typical event.

Symbolic Numbers

Very frequently the numbers found in the Bible have a symbolic value. This is so noticeable that many try to give symbolic meaning to all numbers, searching for mystical significance through complex analysis. Obviously, a great deal of caution should be exercised in attaching such meaning to numbers.

The symbolism of numbers varies widely in published materials according to the viewpoint of the writer. A Spanish-language Jewish encyclopedia, *Enciclopedia Judaica Castellana*, gave the following symbolism of the numbers one to thirteen:

Our God, who is in heaven and on earth, is One. The tables of the law are Two. The patriarchs (Abraham, Isaac, and Jacob) are Three. The mothers of Israel are Four (Sarah, Rebecca, Rachel, and Leah). The books of the Torah are Five. The treatises of the Mishna are Six. The days of the week are Seven. The days till the time of circumcision are Eight. The months of gestation are Nine. The commandments are Ten. The stars (that Joseph saw in his dream) are Eleven. The tribes of Israel are Twelve. The divine attributes are Thirteen.

According to the studies of Ray Summers, numerology played an important part in the apocalyptic writings.

For instance, "1" stood for unity; "2" for strengthening—two people are stronger than one. The number "3" symbolized deity; "4" became the cosmic number of the natural order. "3" plus "4" equals "7"—completeness, combining deity and nature or the whole of existence. The numeral "4" times "3" equals "12"; the Jews saw this as a symbol of organized religion (note the twelve tribes of Israel). Any multiple of "7" or "12" corresponded to the original number. By division "3½" was symbolic of the incomplete. Such phrases as "a time, times, and half a time" and "forty-two months" express a short but indefinite time. Since "6" is one less than "7", it connoted evil—less than perfection. Likewise, "8" is one more than "7", so infinity.[2]

In all this we will note the subjective judgment of the interpreter. Nevertheless, we may be quite sure about the symbolism of a limited series of numbers.

Three usually represents the trinitarian nature of God, that which is divine, and sometimes even that which falsely represents what is divine.

Seven almost invariably represents perfection or what is complete.

Ten is like the number seven; though in some cases both numbers are found in the same context in order to differentiate between them in some way (see Gen. 31:7).

---

[2]Ray Summers, *Worthy is the Lamb* (Nashville: Broadman Press, 1951), quoted by Herschel H. Hobbs in his studies on Revelation.

Twelve suggests the patriarchs, the twelve tribes of Israel, and the twelve apostles. It is doubtful that its symbolic value depends on the multiplication of three by four.

Forty is a symbol of trial or testing, as in the forty years Israel wandered in the desert, the forty days that Moses was on the mountain with God, and the forty days Jesus spent in the wilderness, tempted by the devil.

Thousand and *ten thousand* are round numbers that often, but not necessarily, mean large but indefinite numbers.

The fact that biblical symbols do vary from one text to another requires some study, and more than one biblical reference book should be consulted when investigating a symbol; but the results of this inquiry will help clarify the subject.

For Review

1. Study Proverbs 20:20 in order to determine what is symbolized by the lamp.
2. Study Ezekiel 17 to understand the symbol of the great eagle (see v. 3), the high and lofty mountan (see v. 22), and the birds (see v. 23).
3. In Genesis 40:9–41:32, describe the symbolism of the branches, the baskets, the cows, and the beautiful heads of grain.

15
PARABLES

Jesus' parables are without a doubt the most characteristic feature of His teaching ministry. While our examination of the subject could be much more extensive, we will limit it to three areas: an examination of the parabolic concept, the most important rules for their interpretation, and the application of these rules to several parables in order to illustrate their use.

The word *parable* is derived from two Greek terms: *para*, a preposition meaning "at the side of" or "next to"; and *ballein*, the verb meaning "to throw." Together they indicate something placed alongside something else in order to show the similarity between the two. Briefly, a parable is a story that demonstrates the *likeness* or *similarity* between some common event and an eternal reality.

A parable is much like the simile, except that its details are expanded into a story: a parable is an extension of the simile. It is also a kind of illustration, much like the ones used in a sermon. It is the narration of something that happens in this world, either a bit of history or the story of something that happens often; it is always faithful to human experience. It is told to communicate a spiritual truth.

Without belaboring the point, we should observe that our general use of the term *parable* does not agree completely with its biblical use. In the study of hermeneutics we customarily observe more well-defined limits in classifying the various kinds of figurative language, such as parables, allegories, proverbs, fables, riddles, and enigmas.

The Reason for the Parables

Many of Jesus' parables have an enigmatic character and are not easily understood. As modern readers, we may wonder about this. Even the disciples wondered why Jesus taught using parables or doubted the wisdom of His doing so. They asked Him about it, saying: "Why do you speak to them in parables?" (Matt. 13:10). His answer (see vv. 11–17) gives or implies the following ideas:

- The parable was a very effective means of teaching certain truths to those who were prepared to receive the message of the gospel. Through parables He attempted to overcome the sluggishness of those who were not yet ready to receive it.
- The enigmatic form of the parable was capable of awakening or provoking His hearers so that, at some later time, they would meditate on His words and receive their message.
- The clarity of many parables would serve to convince some hearers in spite of their blindness and rebellion. Those who persisted in not hearing would be without excuse before God.
- The obscure nature of the parable would also serve to hide certain teachings about the kingdom of God

from His enemies, who would eventually bring about His crucifixion.

The Structure of the Parables

The parable is normally composed of three parts: the *occasion*, the *narrative*, and the *spiritual lesson*. In some cases the first and third parts are not given in the biblical account. But we may be sure that in every case there was an appropriate occasion, even though it was not recorded. Jesus taught that way: responding to situations with the proper words. But the Lord did not always point out the spiritual lesson; He sometimes left His hearers to draw it out for themselves.

The Interpretation of Parables

Proper interpretation requires that all three parts of a parable be considered. Any interpretation that turns out to be contrary to the reason why the parable was told, or contrary to the lesson Jesus gave, must be mistaken. This careful examination is the same basic principle as that of considering the context.

A second rule is to understand that *a parable normally teaches only a single truth*, just as the illustration does in a sermon. In every case, study the parable in order to find and express precisely its central teaching. It usually helps to write it out in a single sentence.

A third rule to be considered is this: many details in the parables are included only to describe the human or earthly setting of the story. The details of the setting do not teach something different from the main message of the parable, much less something contrary to the message of the whole Bible. Many interpretations of parables err in this way, forcing some spiritual meaning from every detail and drawing out some teaching foreign to the main message.

This approach to interpretation undoubtedly arose from two sources: first, from the fact that Jesus Himself interpreted two parables for the disciples, apparently teaching that they were to be treated as allegories. Second, the words of Jesus are so highly esteemed that they scarcely allow any detail to be regarded as insignificant. Scholars of the earliest centuries, such as Chrysostom, Theophylac, Origen, and Augustine, readily admitted that the parables taught a single, central message. But they were often so enamored of the beauty of the parables that they violated the principle they professed to uphold. Augustine, for example, "though sometimes laying down the same principle, frequently extends the interpretation through all the branches and minutest fibres of the narrative."[1] This approach to the interpretation of the parables is essentially allegorical. (Allegories will be studied in the next chapter.)

On the matter of determining what is and what is not essential, Trench wrote, "It will help us, if, before we attempt to explain the particular parts, we obtain fast hold of the central truth which the parable would set forth, and distinguish it in the mind as sharply and accurately as we can from all cognate truths which border upon it; for only seen from that middle point will the different parts appear in their true light."[2]

In spite of this emphasis on the central message of the parables, it seems clear that some of the parables

---

[1] Richard C. Trench, *Notes on the Parables of Our Lord* (New York: Appleton, 1854), pp. 32–33.
[2] Ibid., p. 37.

do contain details that are intended allegorically and have meaning that goes beyond the usual secondary place occupied by the details. Such parables would include that of the wicked husbandmen (Matt. 21: 33–44), the marriage of the king's son (Matt. 22:1–14), and others.

The precise rules for recognizing which details are to be understood allegorically are difficult to formulate. Each parable must be read and appreciated for its story and message, and the interpretation of the significant details left to the insight and gifts of the interpreter, as hazardous as this approach may seem. At this point, we trust in the guidance of God's Spirit and an increasing ability for "rightly dividing the word of truth" (2 Tim. 2:15).

One further point: much care should be exercised in the use of parables as the basis for any doctrine, especially when no other texts can be found to support the doctrine which the interpreter would draw from the parable. Of course parables may be used to support doctrines that are affirmed in other parts of the Bible. And points may be drawn from the parables that are not clearly taught elsewhere, if they are not in conflict with the general teaching of the Bible.

One particular example is found in the parable of the faithful and wicked servants (see Luke 12:42–48). In this story the wicked servant thought his master would not return very soon and began to get drunk and beat the other servants; but the master did return and he punished the servant appropriately. The particular points of interest come in verses 47–48: "And that servant who knew his master's will, and did not prepare himself or do according to his will, *shall be beaten with many stripes.* But he who did not know, yet committed things worthy of stripes, *shall be beaten with few.*"

This text undoubtedly teaches that punishment at the judgment will be meted out to those who deserve it, according to their knowledge of God's will and their personal guilt. The parable has a bearing on God's treatment of those who have never heard the gospel message, but it does not clearly indicate what that treatment will be. So far as this writer has been able to discover, there is no biblical teaching directly concerned with those who have never heard the gospel, and it would be a mistake to teach such a doctrine using this parable alone.

The Parable of the Sower (Matt. 13:1-9)

The first parable told by the Lord, and recognized as such by His disciples, was that of the sower. Afterward, in private, His disciples asked Him about its meaning. When He interpreted it for them in detail (see vv. 18-23), He indicated that unless they were able to understand such a simple message, they would not be able to grasp the rest of His teaching. The question Jesus asked the disciples in Mark 4:13: "Do you not understand this parable? How then will you understand all the parables?" was not suggesting that the interpretations that follow would show us how to understand parables in detail. It is simply a mild rebuke of the disciples' spiritual dullness, which would hinder them from understanding His parabolic teaching as a whole.

We will analyze this parable by observing the three parts of its structure.

1. The *occasion* is found in Matthew 13:2. "And

great multitudes were gathered together to Him, so that He got into a boat and sat; and the whole multitude stood on the shore."

It is important to notice the occasion here, because the large crowd undoubtedly included the several kinds of people whom Jesus mentioned in the narrative that follows; the message was for all kinds of people.

2. The *narrative* begins at verse 3 with the words: "Behold, a sower went out to sow" and ends with verse 9, which says: "He who has ears to hear, let him hear!"

In brief, the story is of a man who sowed his seed, letting it fall onto four kinds of soil. We read first of the seed that fell by the roadside and remained on top of the ground, where the birds came and ate it up. Second, part of the seed fell on rocky ground, where the earth was not deep enough to allow the roots to penetrate. The seed sprouted but could not survive under the burning sun. Third, another part fell among thorn bushes, where it was choked and not able to bear fruit. Lastly, some seed fell in prepared ground and gave a harvest of thirty, sixty, and a hundred times the original amount of seed.

Superficially, it might appear that this parable was intended to give four different lessons, though it is really a single parable containing four comparisons; each one agrees with the thrust of the narrative. Its truth may be expressed in a single sentence: The value of the preached Word for the hearer depends on how he listens to it.

3. The *spiritual lesson* is found in the words: "He who has ears to hear, let him hear" (v. 9). This expression may sound to the reader like a simple admonition

to pay attention to the story Jesus had just told; it is that, of course. But the explanation in verses 18–23 shows that the parable deals with the way the four kinds of people who were present in the crowd listen to the Word of God.

The *correct interpretation* in this case, is, of course, the one Jesus gave. But any handling of His interpretation will always consider the three parts of the parable and give the only explanation that will fit them all suitably. It would be highly improbable that any explanation other than the right one could also satisfy those requirements.

On this subject Trench wrote:

Again we may observe that an interpretation, besides being thus in accordance with its context, must be so without any very violent means being supplied to bring it into such agreement . . . (And) it is the proof of the law that it explains all the phenomena and not merely some—that sooner or later they all marshall themselves in order under it: so it is tolerable evidence that we have found the right interpretation of a parable if it leave none of the main circumstances unexplained.[3]

The Parable of the Wheat and Tares (Matt. 13:24–30).

The occasion of this parable is the same as the former. Jesus continued to speak to the crowd using a series of parables, whose general theme was "The Kingdom of Heaven." In this parable the occasion does not affect its interpretation so as to change the character of the message.

---

[3]Ibid., pp. 38–39.

The narrative begins in Matthew 13:24 with the words: "The kingdom of heaven is like a man who sowed good seed in his field," and ends in verse 30 with the words: "but gather the wheat into my barn."

The story is of a man who sowed good seed in his field, only to learn later that an enemy had sown tares on top of the wheat. His servants wanted to pull up the tares, but the farmer delayed them until harvest time. Then he would give instructions to the harvesters to first gather the tares and burn them and then gather the wheat into the barn.

The spiritual lesson does not appear until the Lord Himself explains the parable privately to His disciples (see vv. 37–43) First, He identifies the various persons mentioned in the parable and then explains that it teaches a number of things about the time of the judgment. The Lord will first take away the wicked from the world and cast them into the fire. "Then the righteous will shine forth as the sun in the kingdom of their Father. He who has ears to hear, let him hear" (Matt. 13:43).

The interpretation is found in the words of Jesus in such detail that it leaves nothing lacking. Normally, Jesus spelled out the spiritual lessons for all His hearers as a part of the parable; but in this case the explanation was given to His disciples privately.

Note here that in the two parables explained by the Lord, many of the details have a meaning closely related to the interpretation of the parable. Jesus did not explain all the details, but that does not indicate that their meaning is unclear.

For example, in the parable of the sower, the sower himself is not identified, yet it is clear that the reference is to Jesus. But it also refers to all those who, like Him, sow the seed of the gospel.

Other details clearly have no spiritual counterpart. In the same parable the birds devoured the seed (see v. 4). The meaning is only that the Devil *snatches away* the preached message from the heart and mind of the hearer. While birds eat seeds, the Devil does not eat the message nor derive any benefit from it.

In the parable of the wheat and tares, several details are left unexplained. Nevertheless, most of them have spiritual meaning, though the interpreter ought not to press them for exact correspondence in spiritual matters. The tares were sown "while men *slept.*" Its counterpart is in the fact that the Devil sows bad seed and produces false believers while men are unaware of his activity. Later, the servants of the field's owner ask two questions: where did the tares come from, and would he allow them to pull the tares up immediately. Both questions have their spiritual counterpart in the desire shown by Christians to have answers to vital concerns. Except for Jesus' answer on these points, we might be slow to learn that the Devil plants false believers among the true. And from His answer to the second question, we learn that God will not cut down the false believers right away. They are to grow together with believers until the end, when God Himself will determine which are false and which are His true people.

There are also a few details that have no spiritual meaning. After the two kinds of seed were sown, both sprang up almost simultaneously. No importance should be attached to this. The uprooting of the tares might disturb the wheat and cause it to die; but God's punishment of the wicked would not destroy His saints. So this detail has no direct application to Christians. And the fact that the laborers gathered the tares *into bundles* cannot mean that the angels do the same thing at the time of judgment. This is a detail that belongs only to the earthly narrative.

The following parables are selected as additional examples of the way parables are to be examined, but only because they are well known and readily lend themselves for this purpose.

The Good Samaritan (Luke 10:30–37)

The occasion of this parable is found in verses 25–29, where we read that a certain teacher of the law asked what he should do to inherit eternal life. Jesus turned the question back to him in order to hear his views on the subject. The man answered quoting the commandments of Deuteronomy 6:5 and Leviticus 19:18: "You shall love the LORD your God with all your heart . . . and your neighbor as yourself."

Far from criticizing his response, Jesus approved it, saying: "Do this and you will live" (Luke 10:28). Immediately the teacher tried to evade the force of the commandment, asking for a clarification: "Who is my neighbor?" (v. 29). The parable that follows was given in answer to this second question.

The narrative (see vv. 30–35) is about an unfortunate traveler who was attacked by robbers, relieved of all his possessions, beaten and left half dead on the road. Three people passed by. The first was a Jewish priest, the second was a Levite. Both passed by on the opposite side of the road, thinking, perhaps, that in this way they might escape their duty to the fallen man. The third one to pass by was a Samaritan, a member of the hated race of mixed-blooded Jews. This man had compassion on the wounded man and gave him every possible kind of help, including personal care at an inn and money for his future care.

At this point Jesus asked the teacher of the Law: "Which of these three do you think was neighbor to him who fell among the thieves?" We note here that the important question is no longer "Who is my neighbor?" but "Which of these . . . was a neighbor toward the wounded man?"

The teacher replied correctly that it was the one "who showed mercy on him."

The spiritual lesson is implicit in Jesus' reply: "Go and do likewise." In effect He was saying: "Be a neighbor to anyone who needs you; go and do like that Samaritan."

We note that the answer came, not in response to the question: "What shall I do to inherit eternal life?" but to the other question: "Who is my neighbor?" In this, as in other teachings of Jesus, He puts emphasis on the spiritual manner in which the Jews should fulfill the demands of the law. At the same time He gives an example of the attitude that controls the life of every true child of God.

The Prodigal Son (Luke 15:11–32)

The occasion of this parable is found in Luke 15:1–2. The tax-gatherers and other sinners had come to hear Jesus teach. But when the Pharisees saw them they began to murmur among themselves, "This man receives sinners and eats with them." Seeing their lack of compassion, Jesus related three appropriate parables. Each one illustrated the proper attitude toward the lost: the shepherd rejoiced when he found his lost sheep; so did the woman when she found her lost coin. This third parable is that of a wayward son, illustrating the attitude of his father toward him.

The narrative concerns the younger of two sons,

who wanted to leave his father's home to live in his own way. He asked for and received his part of the inheritance before the proper time, then went a long way off and wasted everything. When he found himself in great need, he remembered his home and decided to return. He arrived repentant and humble. His father saw him a long way off, received him with joy, and began to treat him again as his son.

At this point the story of the repentant son has ended; the father's joyful attitude has been described. The rest of the parable is about the older son, who represents those who would not accept sinners into the kingdom of God. This son approaches the house and is confused by the sounds of rejoicing. Servants tell him that his brother has returned and that his father has received him with a feast. Instead of feeling pleasure over his brother's return, he is angry and refuses to take part in the festivities. His father comes out and begs him to enter, explaining what his attitude toward a repentant sinner should be: "It was right that we should make merry and be glad, for your brother was dead and is alive again, and was lost and is found" (Luke 15:32).

The lesson of the parable is found in these final words. The attitude that the father recommended to his older son is the one the Pharisees should have had. Jesus had already explained that the heavenly Father and the angels rejoice over the repentance of a sinner. Like the shepherd who rejoiced when he found the lost sheep, God rejoices over those who repent and return to Him.

Parabolic Similes and Sayings

Apart from the thirty-four or more parables in the

New Testament, there are a large number of shorter teachings called parabolic similes and sayings. While they are too short to be considered parables in the usual sense, they form an important part of Jesus' parabolic teaching.

The following are examples of *parabolic similes:*

Nor do they light a lamp and put it under a basket, but on a lampstand, and it gives light to all who are in the house. *Let your light so shine before men, that they may see your good works and glorify your Father in heaven* (Matt. 5:15-16).

Can the friends of the bridegroom mourn as long as the bridegroom is with them? *But the days will come when the bridegroom will be taken away from them, and then they will fast* (Matt. 9:15).

No one can serve two masters; for either he will hate the one and love the other, or else he will be loyal to the one and despise the other. *You cannot serve God and mammon* (Matt. 6:24).

Observe here that each parabolic simile contains both a figurative expression and a clear, positive teaching. This combination of the obscure and the clear is characteristic of the parabolic simile. In the verses quoted above, the spiritual lesson is printed in italics.

The *parabolic saying* gives only a figurative teaching without making any explanation in clear language. The parabolic saying requires the hearer/reader to do the interpreting. The following are examples of this type of parabolic teaching:

You are the salt of the earth; but if the salt loses its flavor, how shall it be seasoned? It is then good for nothing but to be thrown out and trampled under foot by men (Matt. 5:13).

You are the light of the world. A city that is set on a hill cannot be hidden (Matt. 5:14).

With the same measure you use, it will be measured back to you (Matt. 7:2).

Let the dead bury their own dead (Matt. 8:22).

Those who are well have no need of a physician, but those who are sick (Matt. 9:12).

In order to facilitate the study of the parables and other parabolic teachings, the following list is included.[4] On comparing the parallel texts the students will find that in some cases a parabolic saying in one will be presented as a parabolic simile in the other.

---

[4]This list is taken principally from Robert C. McQuilkin, *Studying Our Lord's Parables* (Columbia, S.C.: Columbia Bible College, 1938).

Parables	Matthew	Mark	Luke
The two foundations	7:24-27		
The sower	13:2-9	4:2-9	8:4-15
The wheat and tares	13:24-30		
The mustard seed	13:31-32	4:30-32	13:18-19
Blade, head and full grain		4:26-29	
The leaven	13:33		13:20-21
The hidden treasure	13:44		
Pearl of great price	13:45-46		
The dragnet	13:47-50		
The lost sheep	18:12-14		15:1-7
The unforgiving servant	18:21-35		
Workers in the vineyard	20:1-16		
The two sons	21:28-32		
The wicked laborers	21:33-44		
The wedding feast of the king's son	22:1-14		
The budding fig tree	24:32-33		
The thief in the night	24:42-44		
Faithful and evil servants	24:45-51		12:35-40
The ten virgins	25:1-13		
The ten talents	25:14-30		

Parables	Matthew	Mark	Luke
The watchful porter		13:33–37	
The two debtors			7:40–43
The good Samaritan			10:25–37
Friend at midnight			11:5–8
The rich fool			12:16–21
The unfruitful fig tree			13:6–9
The great supper			14:15–24
The lost sheep			15:1–7
The lost coin			15:8–10
The prodigal son			15:11–32
The unfaithful steward			16:1–13
Rich man and Lazarus			16:19–31
The unprofitable servant			17:7–10
The persistent widow			18:1–8
The Pharisee and the tax collector			18:9–14
The ten pounds			19:11–27

Parabolic Similes	Matthew	Mark	Luke	John
Lamp under a bushel	5:15–16	4:21–22	8:16–17	
Cut off your hand	5:30	9:43–44		
Agree quickly with your adversary	5:25–26		12:58–59	
Lamp of the body	6:22–23		11:34–36	
Consider the lilies	6:28		12:27	
Lay not up treasures	6:19–21		12:33–34	
If he asks for bread	7:9–11		11:11–13	
Tree known by its fruit	7:17–20		6:43–45	
Building on rock or sand	7:24–27		6:47–49	
Alms announced with trumpet	6:2–4			
Serve two masters	6:24		16:13	
With what measure ye mete	7:2	4:24–25	6:38	
Foxes have holes	8:20		9:58	
Dead bury their dead	8:22		9:60	
Friends of the bridegroom	9:15	2:19–20	5:34–35	
Harvest is great, workers few	9:37–38		10:2	
Disciple not greater than teacher	10:24–25		6:40	

Parabolic Similes	Matthew	Mark	Luke	John
Children in marketplace	11:16–19		7:31–35	
Sheep (ox) fallen in pit	12:11–12		14:5–6	
Kingdom divided against itself	12:25–26	3:23–26	11:17–18	
Strong man's house robbed	12:28–29	3:27	11:21–22	
Unclean spirit returned	12:43–45		11:24–26	
Household treasures	13:52			
Blind leaders of blind	15:14		6:39	
Whom do kings tax?	17:25–26			
Cleanse outside of vessel	23:25–26		11:39–40	
Budding fig tree	24:32–33	13:28–29	21:29–31	
Watching for the thief	24:42–44		12:39–40	
Shepherd separates sheep and goats	25:32–33			
Entering by narrow door			13:24–30	
Building a tower			14:28–30	
King making war against another			14:31–32	
Wind blows where it will				3:8
Much wood kindled by small fire	James 3:5–6			

Parabolic Sayings	Matthew	Mark	Luke	John
If salt loses savor	5:13	9:50	14:34–35	
City set on a hill	5:14			
Mote in your brother's eye	7:3–5		6:41–42	
Those who are well need no physician	9:12	2:17	5:31–32	
New cloth on old garment	9:16	2:21	5:36	
New wine in old skins	9:17	2:22	5:37–39	
Prophet without honor	13:57	6:4	4:24	
Every plant to be uprooted	15:13			
Bread thrown to dogs	15:26	7:27		
Leaven of Pharisees	16:6	8:15	12:1	
Physician, heal thyself			4:23	
Putting hand to plow			9:62	
Sell coat and buy sword			22:36	
Friend of the bridegroom				3:29
Fields white unto harvest				4:35–38
Slave does not abide forever				8:35
Night comes when no man works				9:4
Walking in the day				11:9–10
If grain of wheat falls into earth				12:24
He who is bathed				13:10
Servant not greater than his lord				13:16; 15:20
Woman who gives birth has pain				16:21

For Review

1. Select two parables not examined in this chapter and identify their various parts.
2. Select several *parabolic sayings* and state the teaching contained in each one.

16
ALLEGORIES

The allegory bears the same relationship to the metaphor and the symbol as the parable does to the simile. As the parable is the amplification of the simile into a narrative, so the allegory is the extension of the metaphor or the symbol into a narrative.

However, the allegory may also take the form of a story whose actors represent something other than their obvious role. This feature at times makes it difficult to distinguish it from the parable.

One significant difference between the parable and the allegory is the number of details with meaning. The allegory offers many more significant details, while the parable has usually a single, central message. Another important difference is that, while the parable is purely imaginary and fictitious, the allegory refers to actual people or events of history.

A simple example of the allegory is found in Genesis 49:9. Note in this case that the allegory begins with a metaphor: "Judah is a lion's whelp." Then the prophet continues his comparison under the same figure:

From the prey, my son, you have gone up.
He bows down, he lies down as a lion;
And as a lion, who shall rouse him?

Other longer allegories are found in the Old Testament, such as that of the vineyard in Isaiah 5:1–7.[1]

The Song of Solomon has most frequently been interpreted as a poetic allegory representing many aspects of the loving relationship between God and His people. More recent studies indicate that it is to be understood as a parable. But again, note the fine line of distinction between the parable and the allegory.

In the New Testament we find, for example, the allegory of the builders and the building (see 1 Cor. 3:10–15). Of special interest is the case of Galatians 4:22–31, which contains the *allegorical use* of the literal history of Sarah and Hagar. And the greater part of the Book of Revelation is composed of a series of allegorical visions.

The first step in interpreting allegories is to study the text carefully, together with any parallel texts, such as those relating to Galatians 4:22–31. The problem is to focus on the principal message. In the case of allegories, the message is more likely to be somewhat diffuse, since the whole narrative is regarded as parallel to the teaching it contains. All the details should be studied to see in what way they contribute to the teaching of the allegory.

Among some interpreters there is the habit of considering the historical facts of the Scriptures to be allegories that convey some "better" teaching. This is the *allegorical method* (see chap. 3). Such interpreters apparently do not consider that the true history contains many useful lessons, and resort to reading history allegorically instead. Others admit the literal

---

[1]This allegory may also be considered as one of the Old Testament parables, because of the overlapping concepts of these two types of figurative language.

sense of the history but insist on adding an allegorical interpretation. In many cases this results in creating a new lesson whose basis is only the interpreters' fertile imagination. We have noted this tendency in the study of types (see chap. 13).

For Review

1. What is the basic metaphor in Psalm 23?
2. Recognizing the ambiguity of verse 6, how would you state the message of the allegory in Proverbs 9:1–6?
3. Study the allegory in Ezekiel 16:1–43 and note how extensively the figure of the prostitute is carried out in the passage.
4. In the allegory of John 15:1–8, note the basic metaphor. Then examine each verse to see what spiritual teaching is derived from the basic metaphor. In verses 7–8, see how the allegorical language blends with the spiritual teaching so as to be almost indistinguishable from it.

17
FABLES, RIDDLES, ENIGMAS, AND PROVERBS

F
our kinds of figurative language will be examined in this chapter: fables, riddles, enigmas, and proverbs.

The Fable

The fable is a fictitious story in which human abilities and characteristics are attributed to nonhuman actors, for the purpose of teaching a moral lesson.

The fable is distinguished from the parable in the *form of the narrative*, and in the *character of its teaching*. The parable teaches only spiritual truth, but the fable never rises to that level; it teaches only moral lessons, with some degree of seriousness. The parable is always a story of human life, either factual or possible; the fable describes animals or inanimate objects that are supposed to have human faculties. For these reasons, personification abounds in fables.

The fable is far more common in secular literature than in the Scriptures; those of Aesop and LaFontaine are typical. And in children's literature, stories of plants, animals, and objects in the natural world, gifted with human capabilities, are very frequent; but they may or may not teach a moral lesson. In the Bible there are very few such stories: perhaps only two can be identified as fables.

One of them is found in Judges 9:7–20, especially verses 8–15. Jotham told this story in which the trees were looking for a king to reign over them. Finally they elected a thorn bush, which proceeded to lay down unbearable conditions for his subjects.

Jotham's reason for telling such a story was to make clear the stupidity of the people in choosing Abimelech as their king and the result of their choice. The fact that God caused an evil spirit to develop between Abimelech and the men of Shechem does not indicate, as some have thought, that the fable had prophetic value in itself. Nevertheless, God's just dealing with the people agreed with Jotham's fable. The story contained a moral principle, which God ratified without affecting the character of the fable.

Another one is found in 2 Kings 14:9–12. Amaziah, king of Judah, wanted to go to battle with Jehoash, king of Israel, whose army was much stronger. By means of the fable Jehoash warned Amaziah not to seek a fight with him. He told the story of the thistle who wanted his son to marry the daughter of the cedar tree. But suddenly a wild beast trampled the thistle.

Jehoash saw the absurdity of Amaziah's invitation to fight with him and used the fable to make it clear. To him it seemed that the battle would be as unequal as the proposed wedding of the thistle and the cedar tree. There is no spiritual lesson in it, only a moral one. When Amaziah did not heed the warning, he was defeated in battle, just as Jehoash had predicted.

The Riddle

In our study of hermeneutics, we need to differentiate between two types of enigma according to the purpose of each kind. The riddle is an enigma that challenges the hearer to solve it. It is most often found in poetic form in the Bible. Also, it is usually told to entertain the hearer and rarely contains any spiritual lesson.

Samson's riddle in Judges 14:14 is famous. The poetic form may be noted in several modern editions; the New International Version translates its poetry best of all:

Out of the eater, something to eat;
Out of the strong, something sweet.

The rhyming of this translation is not part of the original form of the riddle. Hebrew poetry consists of the use of parallelism, a phenomenon we will study in Chapter 18.

The context shows that Samson concocted his riddle to entertain his wedding guests during the days of festivity. He had nothing spiritual in mind. Those who would interpret it as an allegory, referring it to Christ as though it were a prophecy, are clearly mistaken. The only solution to the riddle was the lion and the honeycomb inside its body. The reason the riddle is found in the Bible is to show how God used Samson to punish the Philistines. There is no need to search for a spiritual message.

The Enigma

In contrast to the riddle, the enigma is a truth set forth in obscure language with the immediate purpose of *hiding its truth*; but ultimately, it is intended to awaken the minds of the hearers to think about its meaning.

Usually, if not always, the biblical enigma is intended to present spiritual truth. It is never spoken with the idea of entertaining the hearers. For this reason it will be convenient to keep in mind the difference between the enigma and the riddle, even though the Bible does not always distinguish between the two by using an appropriate word for each. The Hebrew word is *chiydah*, meaning a dark saying, a hard question, a proverb and a riddle (see Num. 12:8). The corresponding Greek word is *paroimía*, a clever or sententious saying, a proverb, or a figurative saying (see John 16:25,29). The term *enigma* is rarely used in any English translation, possibly because the word is not widely understood.

Luke 22:36, a parabolic saying, contains two enigmas: "But now, he who has a money bag, let him take it, and likewise a sack; and he who has no sword, let him sell his garment and buy one."

During the earlier part of Jesus' ministry, He had sent His disciples to preach only among the Jews, who could be expected to provide food and lodging, since the disciples were messengers of the kingdom of God. In that case, they did not need to be concerned about providing for their own living expenses. But now they were to take with them both a purse and a bag of provisions. They could expect to preach the gospel to people who would be their enemies, though this fact was hidden for the moment. In order to hide that truth, Jesus spoke to them using enigmatic language.

He also told them that if they had no sword, they should sell their coat and buy one. But why buy a sword, since the message of the gospel was one of peace and not of violence? And why sell a part of their necessary clothing to buy it? Even though we understand that we are not to use force in preaching the gospel, we must still recognize that the believer often faces dangerous people and situations. Perhaps we are taught that the believer is to be ready to protect himself; if so, always within the law, as the apostle Paul later demonstrated. This enigma does not lose all of its mystery, in spite of possible explanations.

In John 21:18-19 we find another enigma, but there is no difficulty here because verse 19 explains the principal truth.

The Proverb

A proverb is a common saying that is true in itself, but which also expresses a general rule in concrete form. It is used to point out a situation like the one expressed in the proverb. In the Book of Proverbs, however, the exact way they are to be applied is not indicated. There they appear as words of wisdom in capsule form. As such, they came to be practical rules for living.

But proverbs do not always apply as we might suppose. Charles Gore has cautioned us: "A proverb embodies a principle of *common, but not universal*, application in an absolute and extreme form."[1]

Proverbs are to be found in many parts of the Bible, not only in the book by that name. They were often used in daily speech, as in our own times. Matthew 15:26 is a case in point. In answer to the Canaanite woman who asked Jesus to heal her daughter, He replied: "It is not good to take the children's bread and throw it to the little dogs."

---

[1]Charles Gore, *The Sermon on the Mount* (London: John Murray, 1900), p. 87, italics added.

Jesus did not say this to offend her, nor to insinuate that she belonged to a race considered "dogs." His purpose, rather, was to tell her that it was not yet time, in God's plan, to meet the needs of the Gentiles; the Jews must have the gospel offered to them first. But He made this clear by using a common proverb. Jesus had been sent to His own nation, and the Jews should have His ministry before the gospel was preached to others. If the Gentiles were to have it prematurely, it would be like feeding the dogs with the bread that belonged to the children, before they had eaten their meal.

Apparently, the woman did not take offense because she understood the proverb. She knew that children often dropped crumbs to the floor, and threw down larger pieces of bread which they had used to clean their mouths and hands. The dogs under the table ate them up. So she replied, "True, Lord, yet even the little dogs eat the crumbs which fall from their masters' table." She recognized both the truth of the proverb and the Jews' right to hear the message of salvation first. But she insisted on one clear exception: that as the dogs eat the crumbs, a Canaanite woman could receive one small blessing, even while the Jews continued to hear the Lord's message.

Interpreters who do not recognize the presence of a proverb in this conversation will be offended by Jesus' words; they think Jesus was calling this woman a dog. That would be contrary to the gracious spirit of His ministry.

For Review

1. Study the following enigmas and try to understand the truth contained in each one, writing out the

teaching in a single sentence: John 14:12,19,23; 15:26; 16:16.

2. Examine each of the proverbs in the following texts and then state the truth contained in each: 1 Samuel 10:11,12; 24:13; Isaiah 37:3; Ezekiel 16:44; Luke 4:23; 10:11,12.

18
HEBREW POETRY

In a private conversation in Sioux City in 1952, a young man stated boldly that "modernistic churches teach that the Bible contains a lot of poetry." For him, that was the same as saying that liberal Christians believe the Bible does not mean what it says. He understood that poetry consisted of beautiful, exaggerated statements not intended to be taken as truth.

With some difficulty I was able to convince him of the presence of poetry in the Bible, but I had to refer him to his pastor for confirmation of this fact. (I could only hope that his pastor had studied hermeneutics and Hebrew poetry!)

The fact that truth is often stated in poetic form does not diminish its value; rather, the elegance of expression often serves to impress truth more firmly on the minds of those who read it.

One of the important principles of interpretation, especially with regard to the Old Testament, is to recognize the presence of poetry in major portions of the Bible. The poetic section of our Bible is easily recognized; it includes Job, Psalms, Ecclesiastes, and the Song of Solomon. The Book of Lamentations is also completely poetic, even though it has been placed after the Book of Jeremiah, its author.

Because the poetic structure of portions of Scripture provides us with a key to its interpretation, this chapter will be devoted to the study of its characteristics.

Hebrew poetry may have had its origin in the habit of the wise men of the tribes who taught their children orally (see Num. 21:27). By repeating ideas and using different words and phrases, they were able to make their meaning clearer. And with the memorization of those oral traditions, the habit became fixed and associated with the wisdom of the Semitic forefathers.

Whatever the origin of Hebrew poetry, it provided a useful tool for memorizing the Scriptures. Writing on this subject, Anthony C. Deane said,

The chief method employed by the rabbis was to make their pupils learn by heart passages of Scripture, extracts from the "Tradition" and rules of conduct which seemed of special importance. To aid this process, they would arrange the sentences symmetrically, or clothe them in an epigrammatic form, so that they could the more easily be memorized.[1]

The poetry of the ancient Hebrews is different from that of most modern nations, in that the rhyme, rhythm, and assonance in present-day verse do not appear in Hebrew poetry except as accidental features. They occur only in rare cases as matters of curiosity. The principal chararacteristics of Hebrew poetry consist of (1) an elevated and ornate style, (2) the use of special words and grammatical forms, and, most important, (3) a symmetrical form of expression called *parallelism*.

---

[1]Anthony C. Deane, *The World Christ Knew*, 1st ed. (East Lansing, Mich.: Michigan State College Press, 1953), p. 82.

The characteristic called parallelism consists of a certain correspondence between the various lines of the passage, in thought, language, or both. The fact that the same ideas are often repeated in successive lines of poetry, helps in its interpretation in many cases. In Genesis 3:3, for example, we read that the first woman quoted God's commandment as follows:

God has said, You shall not eat it,
nor shall you touch it, lest you die.

Many interpreters have understood these words as the woman's exaggeration of God's commandment. They think she added something to the divine prohibition, something God had not spoken; because we do not find that God had said anywhere: "Nor shall you touch it."

If we recognize that the words of the woman are expressed poetically, we are not likely to understand it as exaggeration. The second phrase is merely the explanation of the first: "You shall not eat it." The words "Nor shall you touch it" mean the same thing: "Do not put your hand on that fruit to eat it." Even in modern speech we may say to a child: "Don't touch it," meaning "Don't eat it, don't steal it, don't bother it, don't play with it," or anything else that the context indicates.

Parallelism is often classified in a number of ways. T. Witton Davies lists seven types: synonymous, antithetical, synthetic, introverted, palilogical, climactic, and rhythmical.[2] *The New Westminster Dictionary of the Bible* adds comparative and progressive parallel-

---

[2]T. Witton Davies in *The International Standard Bible Encyclopedia*, 1st ed., s.v. "Hebrew Poetry."

ism, and omits introverted, palilogical, and rhythmical.[3]For our purpose we will consider five important
types of parallelism.

Synonymous parallelism

In this type, the thought expressed in the first line
is repeated in the following lines, using slightly different language; the vocabulary or grammar may be
changed. This type is very similar to *synthetic* or
constructive parallelism.

In synonymous parallelism, the *structure* of both
parts of the parallelism is the same. The majority of
parallelisms are composed of two lines, though many
have three, four, or even more.

The following are examples of this type. I have italicized the synonymous words or phrases:

For the *upright* will dwell in the land,
And the *blameless* will remain in it (Prov. 2:21).

You are *snared* by the words of your own mouth;
You are *taken* by the words of your mouth (Prov. 6:2).

The floods have *lifted up*, O LORD,
The floods have *lifted up* their voice;
The floods *lift up* their waves (Ps. 93:3).

For He has *founded* it upon the seas,
And *established* it upon the waters (Ps. 24:2).

Does the wild donkey *bray* when it has grass,
Or does the ox *low* over its fodder? (Job 6:5).

Day unto day utters *speech*,
And night unto night reveals *knowledge* (Ps. 19:2).

---

[3]Gehman, *New Westminster Dictionary of the Bible*, pp. 757–8.

Unless the LORD *builds the house*,
They labor in vain who *build* it:
Unless the LORD *guards* the city,
The watchman *stays awake* in vain (Ps. 127:1).

The example quoted earlier in the chapter (Gen. 3:3) is also a synonymous parallelism.

Antithetic parallelism

This type of parallelism repeats the same thought or another like it, by means of a *contrast* or *antithesis*. The Book of Proverbs abounds with this type of expression. In this case, I have italicized the antithetical words or phrases:

Every wise woman *builds* her house,
But the foolish *pulls it down* with her hands (Prov. 14:1).

Righteousness exalts a nation;
But *sin* is a reproach to any people (Prov. 14:34).

The LORD is far from the *wicked*;
But He hears the prayer of the *righteous* (Prov. 15:29).

A *merry heart* does good, like medicine,
But a *broken spirit* dries the bones (Prov. 17:22).

The ox *knows* its owner,
    and the donkey its master's crib;
But Israel *does not know*,
    My people do not consider (Is. 1:3).

With a *little wrath* I hid My face from you for a moment;
But with *everlasting kindness* I will have mercy on you, says
the LORD your Redeemer (Is. 54:8).

These last two examples from Isaiah also demonstrate that poetry is found not only in the "poetic" books but also in others that are predominantly prose. These examples have been printed to show their poetic structure; they do not appear as poetry in the original Hebrew text. This poetic form is provided by the editors of the various translations.

Synthetic or Constructive Parallelism

We may recognize four divisions in this kind of parallelism, as follows:

1. *Corresponding*, in which the expression in the first line is repeated in the second in order to reinforce it, and where the structure of the expression is the same in both members of the *strophe*. (A *strophe* is a poetic couplet or stanza.)
2. *Cumulative*, in which the writer adds several new thoughts after the original one, finally reaching a climax.
3. *Descending scale*, in which the thought is repeated in progressively weaker expressions.
4. *Irregular*, in which the correspondence between the various members of the *strophe* does not follow any of the forms mentioned above.

Here are a number of examples of several types of constructive parallelism. I have shown the primary elements of each paralellism with bold or italic type; you will find other parallel elements as well:

1. *Corresponding*
   The proverbs of Solomon the son of David, king of
      Israel:
   To know *wisdom* and *instruction*;
   To perceive the *words of understanding*,
   To receive the *instruction* of wisdom,

Justice, judgment, and equity;
To give *prudence* to the simple,
To the young man *knowledge* and *discretion*—
A wise man will hear,
    and increase *learning*;
And a man of understanding
    will attain *wise counsel*,
To understand a *proverb*
    and an *enigma*,
The *words of the wise*,
    and their *riddles* (Prov. 1:1–6).

The LORD is **my light** and **my salvation**;
Whom shall I *fear*?
The LORD is the **strength of my life**;
Of whom shall I be *afraid*? (Ps. 27:1).

Let them be **ashamed** and *brought to mutual confusion*
Who *rejoice at my hurt*;
Let them be **clothed with shame and dishonor**
Who *magnify themselves against me* (Ps. 35:26).

2. *Cumulative*
    Seek the LORD **while He may be found**,
        call upon Him **while He is near**.
    Let the *wicked* **forsake his way**,
    And the *unrighteous man* **his thoughts**;
    Let him return to the LORD,
    And He will **have mercy** on him;
    And *to our God*,
    For He will **abundantly pardon** (Is. 55:6–7).

Or why was I not hidden like a stillborn child,
Like infants who never saw light?
There the *wicked* **cease from troubling**,
And there the *weary* **are at rest**.
There the *prisoners* **rest** together;
They do not hear the voice of the oppressor.

> The small and great are there,
> And the *servant* is free from his master (Job 3:16–19).

3. *Descending scale*
   Blessed is the man
   Who *walks not* in the counsel of the **ungodly**,
   Nor *stands* in the path of **sinners**,
   Nor *sits* in the seat of the **scornful** (Ps. 1:1).

   But those who wait on the LORD
   Shall renew their strength;
   They *shall mount up* with wings like eagles;
   They *shall run* and **not be weary**,
   They *shall walk* and **not faint** (Is. 40:31).

4. *Irregular*
   But in my adversity they rejoiced
   And *gathered together;*
   Attackers *gathered* against me,
   And I did not know it;
   They tore at me and did not cease,
   With ungodly mockers at feasts.
   They gnashed at me with their teeth (Ps. 35:15–16).

Poetic Listing

This type of parallelism could be classified as constructive, because it does consist of new ideas added on to the original thought expressed in the first line. Yet, because the ideas are not really related, this type is considered separately. In poetic listing the writer begins with a formula recognizable to readers as a set way of grouping ideas that have little in common. In Proverbs 6:16–19 the writer lists seven things hated by the Lord:

These six things the LORD hates,

Yes, seven which are an abomination to Him:
A *proud look*,
A *lying tongue*,
Hands that shed innocent blood,
A *heart that devises wicked plans*,
Feet that are swift in running to evil,
A *false witness* who speaks lies,
And *one who sows discord* among brethren.

Here is another example:

The leech has two daughters,
Crying, "Give! Give!"
There are three things that are never satisfied,
Four things never say, "It is enough":
The *grave*,
The *barren womb*,
The *earth* that is not satisfied with water,
And the *fire* that never says, "It is enough" (Prov.
30:15–16).

Acrostics

The Hebrew acrostic consists of an arrangement of
lines that begin with the twenty-two letters of the Hebrew alphabet and proceed in alphabetical order.
Psalms 9, 10, 25, 34, 111, 112, 119, and 145 use this arrangement as well as the usual features of Hebrew
poetry. The verses collected under a single letter are
usually isolated sayings without any obvious connection other than their general theme.

Observe especially how Psalm 119 is divided into
"paragraphs" or groups of eight verses. At the head of
each group there is one of the letters of the alphabet:
Aleph, Beth, Gimel, Daleth, etc. This is the only case

where the editors have indicated the acrostic form of the passage. Some versions omit any reference to this feature, notably the Revised Standard Version, the Good News Bible, and the Living Bible.

In addition to these Psalms, the largest part of the Book of Lamentations is written in the acrostic style.

The principal value of using the acrostic was to aid in memorizing a passage of Scripture. A second value would be its artistic form. However, both values are often lost in translation.

For Review

1. Analyze the following texts, classifying each with regard to the kind of parallelism it contains: Proverbs 21:30; 23:29,30; 30:18-31; Ecclesiastes 3:1-8; Isaiah 60:17.
2. In each of the following texts, note what differences of interpretation result when the presence of parallelism is recognized: Hosea 6:6; Proverbs 4:25,26; 8:10; Psalm 19:7-9; Jeremiah 48:10.

19

THE INTERPRETATION
OF PROPHECY

As we examine the interpretation of biblical prophecy, we want to understand the general characteristics of prophecy, its place in the history of Israel and the church, and its ministry to subsequent generations. Ideally, this study also should help us know what to expect with regard to prophecies yet unfulfilled; although the obscure and ambiguous language of prophecy makes it unlikely, in most cases, that anyone could be completely certain about the future acts of the Holy Spirit.

Prophecy and the Prophets

In all prophecy the main concern is the revelation of the will of God with regard to any subject, not merely the prediction of the future. According to the Hebrew word *nābi̅'*, a prophet was simply one who spoke on behalf of another, chiefly for God. In one biblical circumstance (see Ex. 4:16 and 7:1) Aaron is called Moses' prophet. But the word is used overwhelmingly of those who spoke for God with regard to the future, either distant or immediate.[1]

[1]W. Sanday, *Inspiration* (London: Longmans, 1896), p. 84.

Before the word *nābī'* was commonly used to refer to the prophets, they were called "seers," *ro'eh*, as in the days of Samuel (see 1 Sam. 9:9). According to its local usage, this term contained the idea of one who knows secret things, even the future. The prophet combined in himself the abilities of the seer and the preacher.

In the Greek word *prophētēs* there is the basic idea of one who speaks for another. Nevertheless, the prefix *pro* includes the sense of previousness. For this reason the word may be applied to one who speaks of the future. Without a doubt the Hebrews used the word in this sense, as well as the more basic one, to describe the person who spoke for God.

The prophet declared the message he received from God. Whatever the prophet said on God's behalf was prophecy, even though it might not be about the future. Mickelsen expressed this truth when he wrote, "In declaring God's will to the people, the prophet may touch upon the past, the present, or the future."[2] We should also say that the prophet's message with regard to the past was *interpretive*; concerning the present, it was *advisory*; and with regard to the future, it was *predictive*.

Prophets, Messengers for Their Times

Much has been written about understanding the prophets as God's messengers who spoke to the people of their own times. Likewise, there has been insistence on determining the historical situation in order to understand the complete sense of the prophet's message. In this regard, see Chapter 8 on Historical Background. And we must keep in mind that, like preach-

---

ers of our times, the ancient prophets were duty-
bound to speak to the people about their moral obligations to the society in which they lived. They called
the Hebrew people to account for sins of every kind
and offered God's message as the way of salvation.

The great majority of the ancient prophets com-
municated their messages only by the spoken word. A
relatively small number of others wrote out their
messages in order to read or have them read to the
public, frequently in the temple. Then the messages
were fastened to the walls for everyone to read. The
priests or temple assistants would gather, copy, and
preserve them for study by their religious leaders.
Clearly, God had planned that those writings should
remain, not only as writings of importance, but as
part of the Sacred Scriptures. The Spirit of God testified to the truth of these writings and the people understood that the prophecies they contained would be
fulfilled (Matt. 5:18). Their presence in the Bible bears
witness to the great importance of those prophecies
for later times.

The Value of Prophecy

The prophetic word was valuable, first of all, for
those who heard it from the prophet. Through prophecy, God saved or punished His people, according
to the way they responded. The prophet would often
interpret contemporary events, showing that it was
God who brought about those circumstances to chas-
tise His people and bring them to repentance. At the
same time, He provided examples for those who
should come afterwards and prepared them for the
coming of the Savior.

An outstanding example of this predictive function

is Jeremiah's prophecy of the seventy years God's people would spend in captivity. In spite of the fact that their sins had brought that calamity upon them, God promised them salvation and brought it about as He promised. In so doing He preserved the nation as His instrument for bringing the Messiah into the world.

The ancient prophecies should also be considered as revelation intended to guide us in our present-day living. Through them we are better able to understand how to live in this world. On this matter Peter wrote:

We also have the prophetic word made more sure, which you do well to heed as a light that shines in a dark place, until the day dawns and the morning star rises in your hearts (2 Pet. 1:19).

Consequently, the greatest value of the written prophecies was for posterity rather than for the age in which they were written. Their ministry to the people of their own age was relatively brief and limited mainly to those who heard or might be able to read them, while the written history has remained for the use of millions over the course of thousands of years.

The Ultimate Purpose of Prophecy

The most important aspect of the prophetic Scriptures has to do with the Messiah they promised, the message of salvation, and the kingdom of God. We are the beneficiaries of those ancient prophecies. Of this Peter wrote:

To them [those prophets] it was revealed that, not to themselves, but to us they were ministering the things which now have been reported to you through those who have

preached the gospel to you by the Holy Spirit sent from heaven—things which angels desire to look into (1 Pet. 1:12).

The "us" to whom Peter referred were, of course, all
Christian people from Peter's time to our own and until the return of the Lord Jesus Christ. Clearly the principal value of the written prophetic word has to do
with its testimony about the Savior.

Frequently when the prophets delivered their message to the people of their own age, they were guided
by the Spirit to speak of the future, especially of Christ
and His kingdom. In their time the people accepted the
message as for themselves, even though Hebrew com-
munication often contained a notable amount of hyperbole. We do not know to what extent they understood that those prophecies had special reference to
the times of the Messiah. It is possible that a more literal sense was given to the prophecies referring to
Christ and the age to come. For us, it is not hard to
understand that such prophecies spoke specifically of
Christ and only in a limited sense of an era long past.

This phenomenon is often called the "double fulfillment" of prophecy, even though prophecies may have
had not only two, but several applications to later history. Examples of this type of prophecy can be found
in Revelation 6:1–11, Genesis 3:14–16, and Psalm 72.
All of these have a variety of applications or fulfill-
ments.

The possibility that any prophecy should have a
double or multiple fulfillment is completely in line
with the fact that God always guides the history of the
world according to unchanging principles: He deals
with men in righteousness with regard to their sins,
and with mercy when they repent of them. And the re-

sults of their obedience or disobedience are always of the same kind. For this very reason the history of God's dealings with His ancient people serves as a faithful guide for the present. For the same reason the prophecies are valid for the future, because He is the same God dealing with the same kind of people.

Prophecy Contained in Historic Events

Ancient biblical history also had a prophetic character, indicating what the future was to be through various types and prophetic words whose significance was hidden from those who lived it.[3] Even certain obscure points of Israel's history are pointed out in the New Testament as prophecies of Christ. Undoubtedly the writers of those obscure details did not think of them as predictions, though the Spirit later pointed to them as hidden testimonies of Christ.

See, for example, how the evangelist Matthew (see 2:15) applies as a reference to Christ the words: "Out of Egypt I called My son," taken from the prophet Hosea (11:1). In the Book of Hosea the context does not give the slightest hint of speaking of the Son of God who lived for such a brief period in that land. Nevertheless, the prophecy was there and would be fulfilled in due time.

Fulfillment of Prophecy by Stages

Closely related to the phenomenon called "double

---

[3]Because of the prophetic character of those books we now regard as "history," the Jews classified them as "the early prophets." Woven through the text we find warnings, interpretations, advice and predictive messages added to the bare chronological narrative, for the writers were more properly prophets than writers or historians.

fulfillment" is another which we may call the *telescopic aspect* of prophecy. This refers to the fact that prophecy does not often designate the time when its details would be fulfilled. We will be examining certain prophecies that were fulfilled over a long period of time, that is, prophecy fulfilled by stages.

We speak of the telescopic aspect of prophecy because the view it presents is so much like scenery viewed through a telescope. Things that are near or far away seem to be close together; an object that is near at hand may be separated from another by a long distance, but the telescope does not indicate it.

The human eye does not even need a telescope to observe the same phenomenon in the heavens. Stars, moon, and planets seem to be at the same distance from the earth, even though they are often separated by millions of light-years. It appears that the prophets prophesied in the same manner.

There are a number of notable cases in which this phenomenon may be seen. In Isaiah 61:1–2 we read the words that Jesus applied to Himself when He preached in the synagogue at Nazareth:

The Spirit of the Lord GOD is upon Me,
Because the LORD has anointed Me
To preach good tidings to the poor;
He has sent Me to heal the brokenhearted,
To proclaim liberty to the captives,
And the opening of the prison to those who are bound;
To proclaim the acceptable year of the LORD,
And the day of vengeance of our God.

But Jesus read only a part of this text, suspending the reading after the words "the acceptable year of the LORD" (Luke 4:18–19). By doing so, He called attention to His work as one who proclaims "the acceptable year of the LORD." The "day of vengeance" was to be delayed at least by some two thousand years.

The simple fact that He suspended the reading at that point would not be reason enough to affirm that the acceptable year of the Lord and the day of vengeance would be separated from each other. But when we compare the character of His earthly ministry with that of God's judgment at Christ's second coming, the telescopic aspect of the prophecy becomes apparent. We know we live between the two periods mentioned in Isaiah, in the age of Christ's church with its missionary activity in all the nations of the world.

Secular history, too, helps us to see how the telescopic aspect of prophecy has been manifested in the past. In Ezekiel 26 the prophet spoke of the destruction and desolation of the ancient city of Tyre. He said in part:

Therefore thus says the Lord GOD: "Behold, I am against you, O Tyre, and will cause many nations to come up against you, as the sea causes its waves to come up. And they shall destroy the walls of Tyre and break down her towers; I will also scrape her dust from her, and make her like the top of a rock. It shall be a place for spreading nets in the midst of the sea, for I have spoken," says the Lord GOD (Ezek. 26:3–5).

This prophecy began to be fulfilled in 598 B.C. when Nebuchadnezzar (see verse 7) besieged the part of the city that was built along the edge of the Mediterranean. During the thirteen years that followed (until 585 B.C.), the coastal city was defeated and completely destroyed. Apparently the prophecy of Ezekiel had been fulfilled, even though not in such detail as stated in the prophecy.

Yet an important part of the city remained intact after Nebuchadnezzar's siege. Tyre was composed of two parts: one part lay along the shore for some seven miles, but the most important part was on an island about a mile long, half a mile from shore. Though Nebuchadnezzar destroyed the city on the mainland, he was not able to do anything against the island city.

In 322 B.C. (263 years later) Alexander the Great came, after having conquered all the people in his path. For fear of him, the inhabitants of the island city of Tyre accepted his sovereignty but would not allow him personally to come inside the city gates. Alexander was so enraged by this insult that he decided to force his way in. For nine months the inhabitants of the city defended it successfully. Finally Alexander accomplished his purpose after building a kind of isthmus between the shore and the island. He used the rubble of the ancient city, scraping the earth for every available bit of material and throwing it into the water. With the new foothold he was able to force his way into the city.

As a result of Alexander's efforts, the island city was turned into a "bare rock," and today the isthmus is "a place for the spreading of nets in the midst of the sea." The city has never been rebuilt and its population has stayed the same, never passing beyond some five thousand inhabitants.

In this case we see how prophecy is sometimes fulfilled in stages.

Direct and Indirect Prophecies of Christ

Of special interest are the *direct prophecies* of the Messiah, as contrasted with the *indirect* prophecies of Him. *Direct* prophecies are those that refer clearly and uniquely to Christ, without mentioning any other person or historical circumstance. There is no fulfillment of them other than in Christ. *Indirect* prophecies are those that refer primarily to another person or historical circumstance, but *whose language can be fulfilled perfectly only in Christ.*

Observe the difference between the two prophecies that follow:

Awake, O sword, against My Shepherd,
Against the Man who is My Companion,
Says the LORD of hosts.
Strike the Shepherd,
And the sheep will be scattered (Zech. 13:7).

Therefore my heart is glad,
and my glory rejoices;
My flesh also will rest in hope.
For You will not leave my soul in Sheol,
Nor will You allow Your Holy One to see corruption (Ps. 16:9,10).

Jesus applied the first of these to Himself (Matt. 26:31); history does not indicate any other person who might have been in the prophet's mind. For present-day readers, the language of the prophecy leaves no doubt that the reference is to the crucifixion of Christ.

The second of the two prophecies cited above is applied by the apostle Peter to Christ's resurrection (Acts 2:25–31). In expounding the prophecy Peter recognized that the basic reference was to King David, though some of the details David mentioned were not fulfilled in his own person. For this reason, said Peter, and because David was a prophet, the words must be understood as referring to Christ. This is an *indirect* prophecy.

In the interpretation of any prophecy of Christ, we should examine carefully the historical setting in order to know whether it is to be understood directly or indirectly of Him. Once it has been determined that a prophecy is directly concerned with Him, we should not insist on finding an immediate application to some ancient person or event. At the same time, we should be open to the possibility that further study might show a genuine historical reference.

Prophecy in the Contemporary Life of Israel

Though for us the principal value of the ancient prophecies is its messianic aspect, the Old Testament abounds in prophecies related to the contemporary life of Israel and neighboring nations. By this kind of prophetic word, God governed His people, guiding them in war, protecting them from danger, and reproving them of sin.

Israel was given the means of knowing when the prophetic words were to be believed. If a certain prophecy was spoken on behalf of God and it was fulfilled, it was of God; if not, it was not of God. This was the instruction:

But the prophet who presumes to speak a word in My name, which I have not commanded him to speak, or who speaks in the name of other gods, that prophet shall die. And if you say in your heart, "How shall we know the word which the LORD has not spoken?"—when a prophet speaks in the name of the LORD, if the thing does not happen or come to pass, that is the thing which the LORD has not spoken; the prophet has spoken it presumptuously; you shall not be afraid of him (Deut. 18:20–22).

Such instructions were a useful warning to the people to whom they were given. Here are a few examples of prophecies that were spoken only a short time before their fulfillment:

- The flood in Noah's time was prophesied (see Gen. 6:13–18). Without a doubt Noah made it known to the people.
- The defeat and death of Saul were prophesied by Samuel (see 1 Sam. 28:16–19).
- Daniel prophesied the transfer of Belshazzar's kingdom (see Dan. 5:25–28) and it happened as described by him (see vv. 30–31).
- Jeremiah prophesied the seventy years of captivity (see Jer. 25:11) and it came to pass (see Dan. 9:2).

In the New Testament we see other examples:
- Jesus prophesied that the disciples would be scattered the night He was betrayed (see Matt. 26:31) and it happened (see v. 56).
- Jesus said that Peter would deny Him that same night (see Matt. 26:34) and he did (see vv. 74–75).
- He also said that Judas would turn Him over to the authorities (Matt. 26:23–25), and it was true (vv. 48–49).
- Agabus prophesied Paul's arrest in Jerusalem (see Acts 21:11), and it took place as predicted (see v. 33).
- Paul himself prophesied the safety of those who traveled with him in the ship, even though the ship would be lost (see Acts 27:22–26), and their lives were spared (see v. 44).

Figurative Language in Prophecy

In certain cases the poetic and figurative language may obscure the prophetic meaning of a passage. Both forms may be observed in the first prophecy concerning Christ (see Gen. 3:15). The same features will be seen also in the larger context, verses 14–19. Verse 15 reads:

And I will put enmity
Between you and the woman,
And between your seed and her Seed;
He shall bruise your head,
And you shall bruise His heel.

The reader will notice that these lines are arranged in *poetic* form. Note, too, that God speaks here *figuratively* as well as poetically.

Even though the serpent was literally a "beast of the field" (v. 14), it was also a *symbol* of Satan. When God spoke of the seed of the serpent and of the woman, He used a *metonymy* that suggests the descendants of both. The seed of the serpent would be the children of the Devil, but the Seed of the woman would be Jesus, the Son of Mary. The wound on the serpent's head is a metonymy for the destruction of Satan's power. And in the same way, the wound on the heel of the woman's Seed suggests the less significant physical harm done to Jesus at the crucifixion.

Because there is much figurative language in prophecy, it should not surprise us that its fulfillment may not be in literal, historical events but only in unseen, spiritual events. See the following case:

For you shall go out with joy,
And be led out with peace;

The mountains and the hills
Shall break forth into singing before you,
And all the trees of the field shall clap their hands.
Instead of the thorn shall come up the cypress tree,
And instead of the brier shall come up the myrtle tree;
And it shall be to the LORD for a name,
For an everlasting sign that shall not be cut off (Is.
55:12–13).

The words that say that the mountains and hills
would break forth into singing and that all the trees
would clap their hands are clearly figurative. Through
personification these features of nature are represented as sharing the joy of the children of God, according
to the words of the first line; in a single prophecy we
have both literal and figurative language. So we are
led to expect that the fulfillment of the words about
the mountains and hills and the trees will be spiritual.
We use the context to understand whether the sense of
the words is literal or figurative, and then give them
the appropriate interpretation.

Of course, not all prophecy was written or spoken
in poetic language, nor is there figurative language in
every prophecy. Still, poetry and figurative language
are some of its common characteristics, and we must
be prepared to recognize their presence in prophecy.
The fulfillment of some prophecies or of their details
must be understood figuratively.

Rules for Interpreting Prophecy

1. Keep in mind that the true interpretation of any
   prophecy remains with God, since all prophecy
   originated with Him. For this reason no one may

interpret "privately," but only in agreement with the message of the rest of prophecy.

2. Whatever interpretation is given by the Scriptures themselves must be accepted in place of any other of human origin.

3. Remember that the guiding spirit of prophecy is that of bearing testimony to Jesus as the Christ (see Rev. 19:10).

4. Observe that prophecies often have more than one fulfillment, and that these may be both immediate and remote.

5. Note, too, that the several elements of any prophecy may be fulfilled at times greatly separated from each other.

6. Remember that prophecy is often composed of both poetic and figurative language, as well as that which is prosaic and literal. Poetic and figurative language must be interpreted by their own set of rules.

7. The interpretation of any prophecy may be either literal or figurative, according to the character of its language and of its larger context.

For Review

1. Examine the prophetic passages listed below in detail and identify the various characteristics mentioned in this chapter.
   Deuteronomy 18:15–22
   2 Samuel 7:10–16
   Psalm 22
   Isaiah 7:13–17
   Isaiah 52:13–53:12

20
SCRIPTURAL
QUOTATIONS

These final chapters will be devoted to special problems of biblical interpretation, not covered as figurative language. These include the difficulties that arise from the inexact quotations from the Old Testament in the New; discrepancies between events mentioned in the Bible and evidence from the secular world; and problems that believers have with biblical doctrines.

The difficulties we will look at in this chapter are the discrepancies between certain Old Testament texts and the way they are quoted in the New Testament. This is no small problem when we understand that there are 263 direct quotations from the Old Testament in the New, and some 376 indirect quotations.

For those who have accepted the biblical teaching of the complete inspiration and inerrancy of the Scriptures, this kind of difficulty may be perceived as a threat to their faith. When a problem is not explained easily, it is tempting to question either the truth of the sacred text or its inspiration. It is necessary, therefore, to face frankly the difficulties found in the text and to solve them if possible. The purpose of this study will be to try to explain the reasons for the discrepancies and to demonstrate that they do not affect either the truthfulness of the Scriptures or the evangelical concept of their complete inspiration.

The Origin of Old Testament Quotations

Generally speaking, the quotations from the Old Testament were taken from the Septuagint, the "Version of the Seventy," often referred to by the Roman numerals LXX. This was the translation of the Hebrew Old Testament into Greek, made by a group of Jewish scholars—seventy, according to the tradition—who were resident in Alexandria, Egypt. The translation was done about two centuries before Christ. It appears now that the LXX was translated from Old Testament manuscripts that varied somewhat from the manuscripts later adopted as part of the recognized canon of Scripture. This final selection was made between A.D. 70 and 100.[1]

The Jews of the Dispersion normally used this Septuagint version for reading, study, and memorization. It was natural, then, that the writers of the New Testament should use this Greek text whenever they quoted from the Old Testament; both because they knew it by heart and because they were writing in Greek.

Sometimes the New Testament writers felt it was necessary to quote texts from the Hebrew original, making certain changes in the LXX reading because they found it necessary to correct the reading at those points.

With great frequency the writers tried to give the *sense* of the original text rather than quoting the Old Testament with verbal accuracy. When they did that,

---

[1]Eduard Lohse, *The New Testament Environment*, p. 92.

we cannot properly attribute this to inaccuracy. Instead we should classify such quotations as *approximate*, *indirect*, or perhaps only as a *reference* to the original, which does not pretend to translate or quote it with verbal accuracy.

The tendency to quote with inexactness is illustrated in John 13:10–11. Jesus says in this place: "You are clean, but not all of you." But in the next verse John quotes the same words of Jesus in another way: "Therefore He said: 'You are not all clean.' " It is evident that the writer was not verbally accurate in repeating the direct quotation, though he quoted Jesus' words with *complete truthfulness* as to the content of the statement. There is nothing added or missing from the second form of the statement. The difference in the two quotations may be due to the writer's wish to avoid the monotonous sound of the exact repetition of the words immediately after their first appearance.

This case illustrates clearly that the Evangelists did not insist on verbal exactness when they quoted the words of another person, even the words of Christ Himself. The same custom was evidently used in quoting the Old Testament in the New.

Sometimes quotations are more precisely taken from the original Hebrew text. Matthew, for example, who normally takes his quotations from the Septuagint, goes to the Hebrew text as the source when he refers to the Messiah.

In some cases the quotations are *paraphrased*, or restated in a form that is very much abbreviated. Psalm 78:2–3 says:

I will open my mouth in a parable;
I will utter dark sayings of old,

Which we have heard and known,
And our fathers have told us.

Matthew quoted it in an abbreviated form:

I will open My mouth in parables;
I will utter things which have been
kept secret from the foundation
of the world (Matt. 13:35).

The fact that it is abbreviated is not important since he merely quotes a part of the original statement. But he has changed the singular "parable" to "parables" and substituted a clarifying clause for the words "dark sayings of old." This has become: "Things which have been kept secret from the foundation of the world."

Some quotations are really *combinations of several texts.* For example, Mark 1:2–3 reads as follows:

Behold, I send My messenger before Your face,
Who will prepare Your way before You.
The voice of one crying in the wilderness:
"Prepare the way of the LORD,
Make His paths straight."

This quote combines Malachi 3:1:

Behold, I send My messenger,
And he will prepare the way before Me,

and Isaiah 40:3:

The voice of one crying in the wilderness:
Prepare the way of the LORD;
Make straight in the desert
A highway for our God.

Variant Wording of Original Texts

As stated earlier, the variations between the LXX and the New Testament quotations from it are partly due to the fact that the writers wanted to make the Septuagint reading agree with the Hebrew original, or to give emphasis to some special point of their argument.

In other cases the variations are due to the fact that *the New Testament writers read the Hebrew text differently* from the LXX translators. Due to the form of the Hebrew language, it was possible to read the text more than one way in some cases.

Ancient Hebrew words were written only with consonants and one or two vowels. Normally the vowels were supplied by the reader, and in some cases readers supplied the wrong ones. Some consonants were confused because of their similar appearance: the *Daleth* and *Resh*, *Yodh* and *Vav*, *He* and *Cheth*. The copyists, too, sometimes made mistakes and produced manuscripts that were not exact copies of the originals. The study of specific passages must be left to students of Hebrew who are concerned about this problem.

Approximately one-half of the quotations of Old Testament texts *emphasize the sense of the original* rather than give word-for-word equivalents. This may be seen easily in the rendering of Isaiah 11:10. The prophet wrote:

And in that day there shall be a Root of Jesse,
Who shall stand as a banner to the people;
For the Gentiles shall seek Him,
And his resting place shall be glorious.

Paul gave only the sense of this passage in Romans 15:12:

There shall be a root of Jesse;
And He who shall rise to reign over the Gentiles,
In Him the Gentiles shall hope.

In other cases the New Testament form of the quotation may depend on the *meaning of the words in the Hebrew text.* In Genesis 22:18 God had said to Abraham: "In your seed all the nations of the earth shall be blessed." However, in Galatians 3:16 Paul appealed to the singular sense of the word "seed" as the basis for saying that the promises of God were given to Abraham and his seed (singular), that is, to Christ: "He does not say, 'And to seeds,' as of many, but as of one, 'And to your Seed,' who is Christ." It is often said that Paul's argument in this place has no real basis because the word "seed" in Hebrew (*zera'*) is used collectively for "seeds," plural. This is certainly true, as is also the case with the Greek word for seed (*sperma*); but the singular sense was determined to be the correct one by the translators of the Septuagint. Consequently they chose the singular *spérmati* in place of the plural *spérmasin*, obviously a deliberate choice. Paul's appeal to it was no mere rabbinic hair-splitting; he confirmed the Septuagint at this point and based his argument upon it.

There are, of course, other cases where appeal is made to a particular sense of the Hebrew as the basis for a change in the New Testament rendering of the passage.

In some cases the reason for the changes is very evident; they are necessary for adjusting the grammatical form of the original text to the new context, changing its number, person, tense, or voice.

Sometimes the Old Testament quotation is changed to present a special argument or to bring out a new thought, giving a limited sense to the Hebrew word. In Psalm 97:7 the writer wrote, "Worship Him, all you gods." But the writer of Hebrews quoted it differently: "Let all the angels of God worship Him" (Heb. 1:6). In this case, the writer points to one of several meanings of the word *elohim*, translated literally "gods." (The word may also mean "God," "sons of God," "angels," or "judges.")

Other variations are due to the *use of synonymous expressions* in place of verbal equivalents. In Romans 15:12 (mentioned above) where Paul quoted Isaiah 11:10, he used the expression "He who shall rise to reign over the Gentiles," whereas the original read, "Who shall stand as a banner to the people."

In a number of places the variations are so different that special explanations are in order. One of these, Hebrews 10:5, is taken from Psalm 40:6. The writer of Hebrews quoted the passage from Psalms this way:

Sacrifice and offering You did not desire,
But a body You have prepared for Me.
In burnt offerings and sacrifices for sin
You had no pleasure.
Then I said, "Behold, I have come—
In the volume of the book it is written of Me—
To do Your will, O God."

The words of Psalm 40:6, which are of special interest, say: "My ears You have opened," but are translated in Hebrews 10:5 as: "But a body you have prepared for me."

B. F. Westcott, commenting on this change, wrote, "The King, the representative of men, recognizes in the manifold organs of His personal power—His body—the one fitting means for rendering service to God. Through this, in its fullness, He can do God's will."[2]

Another possible explanation is that the word "body" is substituted for "ear." In the earliest manuscripts, which were written in large characters called "uncials," the word *soma*, body, could easily be mistaken for *otia*, ear; an examination of the Greek letters will show that this could happen. However, this limited explanation leaves too much else to the imagination.

A better explanation is that the word "opened" in the Hebrew is literally "pierced." "Opening the ear" may be taken as a reference to the custom of piercing the ear as a sign of voluntary servitude for all of one's life (see Ex. 21:6). In this case, the Hebrew expression: "Mine ears hast thou opened" is considered to mean: "Thou didst accept me as a voluntary slave."

It should be underscored that any reading the apostolic writers took from the LXX and used in the New Testament, was quoted by divine authority, since the New Testament writers worked by the inspiration of God's Holy Spirit. Whatever questions we may raise as to the precise way in which the words found their way into the New Testament text, these questions should not hinder their full acceptance as bearing the message of the Spirit of God.

There are also a number of texts whose Old Testament origin has not been determined. Matthew 2:23,

---

[2]B. F. Westcott, *The Epistle to the Hebrews* (New York: Macmillan, 1906), p. 311.

where Jesus was called a Nazarene, is said to be the teaching of "the prophets." The closest we can come to identifying the source is to refer to Isaiah 11:1, which said the Messiah would be a righteous "branch" (Hebrew, *nēzer*); the name *Nazareth* came from the same Hebrew root.

Ephesians 5:14 may be based on Isaiah 60:1. Paul wrote, "Therefore He says: 'Awake, you who sleep,/ Arise from the dead,/And Christ will give you light.' " Isaiah said, "Arise, shine;/For your light has come!/ And the glory of the LORD is risen upon you." However, Paul may not mean "He (Christ) says," or "It (the Scripture) says," but "He (the Spirit) says." In this case it would not be a quotation from Scripture. Many scholars believe Paul was quoting a first-century hymn sung at baptism. The presence of the word "Christ" in the text, makes it most unlikely that the quotation comes from the Old Testament.

Jude 9 and 14 are taken from Hebrew apocalyptic writings that were not accepted as part of the inspired canon. Apparently Jude quoted from the extra-canonical book *Ascension of Moses* in the first case, and from the *Book of Enoch* in the second. Again, the apostolic use of these words assures us that these particular words are from God, if not from recognized books of the Bible.

Acts 20:35 quotes one of Jesus' sayings that was preserved for us by oral, apostolic tradition: "It is more blessed to give than to receive."

And there are certain quotations from secular literature. Acts 17:28 and Titus 1:12 include Paul's quotations from the works of Greek and Roman writers. Naturally these quotations have no authority other than that which is given them by virtue of their use by Paul.

Guidelines for Interpreting Old Testament Quotations

1. The great majority of Old Testament quotations in the New Testament come from the Septuagint.

2. No one maintained the verbal inspiration of the Septuagint, since it was but a Greek version of the Scriptures. Consequently, the New Testament writers felt at complete liberty to modify it whenever they chose to do so.

3. Jewish writers did not recognize the obligation to quote others with literal exactness. Yet the inexactness that appears in the text does not affect the truthfulness of the quotations.

4. The writers of the New Testament knew large portions of Scripture from memory and were familiar with much more than that. When they did not have the written Scriptures at hand, they undoubtedly used their memory to quote them.

5. The New Testament *as it stands* is the work of the Holy Spirit, even though we may not know the exact reasons for its many variations in quoting Old Testament passages.

For Review

In the light of the discussions of this chapter, examine the following texts and try to determine the possible reasons for the variations they present:

1 Corinthians 2:9, cf. Isaiah 64:4.

1 Corinthians 15:45, cf. Genesis 2:7.

Romans 9:25, cf. Hosea 2:23.

Romans 11:8, cf. Isaiah 29:10 and Deuteronomy 29:4.

21
HISTORICAL
CONTRADICTIONS

The topic of historical contradiction within the Bible and between the Bible and other written records has received a great deal of attention. The wonder is that the Bible presents so few difficulties, since its various books were written at such different times and places.

The Bible consists, it may be answered, of many separate books. Their origin is manifold. The languages in which they were composed are disused; they are distinct from each other, and different from our own. The expressions, images, and thoughts that the Bible contains belong to different ages, countries, and persons; the manners and customs it describes have passed away; its topics are the most various and comprehensive, including the history, in part, of all nations and all times; and it contains disclosures and precepts which refer to both worlds, expressed necessarily in terms taken from one only; and the whole revelation is included in a brief volume. Let these and kindred facts be remembered, and it will be seen at once that, to give, within so narrow a range, and even to give at all, to mortal, finite minds, a revelation that shall be free from difficulty is impossible. Difficulties there must be, such as need a larger amount of inquiry than any one man can give, and such as will leave, after the utmost inquiry, much to be explained.[1]

---

[1]Joseph Angus and Samuel G. Green, *The Bible Handbook* (London: Religious Tract Society, 1905), pp. 259–260.

It should be noted that many of the so-called biblical contradictions are unreal. In numerous cases the
difficulty disappears after careful study of the text has
clarified exactly what it says. Some contradictions are
solved by better translations of the original. In other
cases, knowledge of the customs of the people and of
the time and place where that part of the Bible was
written will eliminate the problem.

The present study will be devoted to examining a
number of typical difficulties, which are frequently
called "historical contradictions." When we look at
this kind of problem we should keep several thoughts
in mind.

1. Some accounts that appear to be contradictory reports of an event are really reports of different events.
The two genealogies of Jesus (see Matt. 1:1–16 and
Luke 3:23–38) include a series of different names. It is
very possible that the two genealogies are those of the
two parents: that of Joseph in Matthew and that of
Mary in Luke. The latter possibility is based on the
curious expression in Luke 3:23: "being (*as was supposed*) the son of Joseph, the son of Heli." In this case
it is necessary to read the verse this way: "being the
son of Mary, the daughter of Heli." Even though nothing can be proved on this matter, Frederic Godet supports this interpretation of the facts. We know, furthermore, that there was a very old tradition that
affirmed that Mary was of Davidic lineage, like Joseph. The Talmud also refers to Mary as the daughter
of Heli.[2]

The call of the apostles in Matthew 4:18–22 and

---

[2]Louis Matthews Sweet in *The International Standard Bible Encyclopedia*, s.v. "Genealogy of Jesus Christ."

Luke 5:1–11 differs from the call mentioned in John 1:35–42, with regard both to the time and place where it happened. The call mentioned in John refers to the invitation Jesus gave them to follow Him personally, while the ones recorded in Matthew and Luke deal with His call to apostolic service.

The "Lord's Prayer" was undoubtedly given on two separate occasions: the first time was before the multitude (see Matt. 6:9–15). The second time was to the disciples, privately (see Luke 11:2–4).

2. When the Gospel writers recorded the same story, they sometimes gave us different details. A longer narrative from one Gospel may include a shorter narrative from another Gospel, but the shorter one does not contradict the longer.

The two stories of Jesus' childhood differ considerably without contradicting each other; they coincide at Matthew 2:22–23 and Luke 2:39. Luke omits the story of the period Jesus' family spent in Egypt.

In the narrative of the demon-possessed men (see Matt. 8:28–34, Mark 5:1–20, and Luke 8:26–39), Matthew mentions two of them; but Mark and Luke speak only of one. Most likely, Mark and Luke single out one of the men as being the important one in the story, without mentioning the second one. The number of demons is clearly many in all the narratives.

3. When different accounts are given of what was said on a particular occasion, one may give the exact words while the other records only a part of the conversation or discourse. Perhaps the writer varied the order of the words according to his own editorial purpose or plan, or felt that only the *sense* of the words was necessary.

Note the two forms of the Sermon on the Mount

(see Matt. 5–7 and Luke 6:17–49). Matthew reported it more completely, while Luke gave us only a synopsis. With regard to the place where Jesus preached that sermon, Matthew said Jesus went up into the mountain, but Luke said He came down from the mountain to a level place. That level place was probably part of the mountain, a ledge or small meadow above the valley but below the place where Jesus had prayed all night (Luke 6:12–16).

4. Some narratives use *general expressions* whose meanings are modified or defined by more exact statements in other accounts. Note again that whatever is obscure and difficult should be explained by other statements, which are clear and easy to understand.

The instructions given to the disciples when they were sent out to preach, differ in the three synoptic Gospels. The exact way in which they differ may be seen by comparing the items the disciples were to carry on their evangelistic tour:

Matthew 10:9–10	Mark 6:8–9	Luke 9:3
. . . .	nothing for the journey	nothing for the journey
no gold nor silver, nor copper	no copper in their money belts	nor money
nor bag	no bag	nor bag
nor two tunics	not to put on two tunics	do not have two tunics
nor sandals	wear sandals	. . . .
nor staffs	except a staff	neither staffs
. . . .	no bread	nor bread

Mark's narrative, which says the disciples should wear sandals and carry a staff, apparently contradicts the other two, which say these articles were not to be taken. The prohibition of these two items is not an exact expression, but a general one with its exceptions as Mark indicates. We should understand that since Jesus told the disciples not to take two sets of clothing, He also meant they were not to take *extra* shoes and staff, according to the phrase "nothing for your journey," repeated by both Mark and Luke. But Mark, recording the instructions from Jesus with greater accuracy, makes them clearer: the disciples were to wear sandals and carry a staff to help them walk. Undoubtedly it was understood that they were not to carry *extra* shoes and staffs. This interpretation is underscored when we note the plural form "staffs" in both Matthew and Luke.

The biblical narratives were written according to different plans and for different purposes. Some accounts follow the chronological order of events, while others group narratives according to some theme or for a specific purpose. Determining the editorial plan of each book helps to harmonize the differences in the history they relate.

Nevertheless, the reader will not find perfect consistency within the plan of any one writer. For example, Mark and Luke usually follow a chronological plan, while Matthew groups narratives according to subjects. But sometimes the plan is reversed: Matthew is chronological while Luke will group events by subject.

We note this change in Matthew 4:3–11 which contains the story of Jesus' temptation and states the exact order of the events. Luke gave them a different order (see Luke 4:1–13).

Genesis 1:27 mentions briefly the creation of man; then in 2:7–23 the writer recounts this event in more detail, as being worthy of special attention. They are not to be viewed as conflicting stories; the second merely enlarges upon the first.

In some cases there seems to be a discrepancy between the original history and the reference made to it in another part of Scripture. In Mark 2:26 Jesus says that David and his men "went into the house of God in the days of Abiathar the high priest." But 1 Samuel 21:1 says that Ahimelec was high priest at that time. The difficulty may be resolved in this way: Abiathar was the son of Ahimelec. When King Saul had Ahimelec killed, Abiathar escaped, fled to David, and was made high priest. Since Abiathar was more prominent in Israel's history than his father Ahimelec, it was natural to refer to "the days of Abiathar" rather than to the times of his father. Thus, it was literally true that David entered the house of God *in the days of Abiathar,* though not while he was high priest.

In Galatians 3:17 Paul wrote that 430 years had passed from the time when the promise was made to Abraham until the time God gave His people the Ten Commandments. However, according to Exodus 12:40 Israel was *in Egypt* for 430 years. Abraham had received the promise more than 200 years before Jacob and his family went to Egypt; so the total length of time from the Abrahamic covenant to the Exodus was 630 years, not 430.

Apparently Paul calls attention to the fact that the promise was given equally to the three patriarchs, "Abraham, Isaac, and Jacob," but since Abraham was the first one to receive it, he alone is mentioned by name. Then Paul spoke of the 430 years to specify the length of time between the giving of the promise *to the patriarchs,* and the giving of the law at Mount Sinai. Paul was not speaking of Abraham as an *individual,* but of *the patriarchal age.* That age ended with Jacob, some 200 years after Abraham.

Sometimes a biblical reference to an earlier history provides more information than the original account of an event or period.

Psalm 105:18 says that Joseph's feet were "hurt with fetters; he was laid in irons," where the Genesis narrative does not mention this detail, according to the usual translations. But the word "prisoners" in Genesis 39:20 means literally "those who are bound or in chains." Joseph was put in prison with other prisoners who were bound or in chains, and we must assume that he was bound in the same way.

The saying attributed to Jesus in Acts 20:35, "It is more blessed to give than to receive," does not appear in any of the four Gospels. Without a doubt it was part of the oral apostolic tradition.

The marriage of Salmon to Rahab (see Matt. 1:5) is not included in the Old Testament history. This detail seems to have been a part of an ancient oral tradition; it was not customary to include the names of the wives in the genealogies.

In each of these cases the Old Testament writers did not include all the details in their narratives. The New Testament writers may have gotten their information from unknown written sources or from oral tradition; and some believe that they received this information by revelation.

Certain facts related in the Bible do not agree with secular history; but many of these problems are solved with careful study. In this category belong variations in historical dates and in personal and place names. In many cases the biblical narrative has been confirmed by means of archaeology or other scientific investigations. Other discrepancies remain, many of which will undoubtedly be resolved as further research is done.

For Review

Examine the supposed contradictions listed below. Then look at the various approaches to this kind of problem to find an appropriate solution.

Genesis 1:1–2:3 and Genesis 2:4–25
Exodus 33:11 and John 1:18
Matthew 16:17–19 and 1 Corinthians 3:11
Matthew 26:34 and Mark 14:30

22
DOCTRINAL
DIFFICULTIES

On a certain occasion a cynic asked the humorist Mark Twain what he did with all the things in the Bible he could not understand. Twain replied to the effect that the things he did not understand didn't bother him; what bothered him were the things he *did* understand!

Many of the objections to the Bible, both for unbelievers and even for many Christians, is what the Bible teaches on certain difficult topics. Perhaps these difficulties are more serious than the supposed historical and scientific contradictions.[1]

Doctrines such as original sin, the condemnation of the human race to eternal death, the bondage of the human will, salvation by grace, the substitutionary death of Christ, and the bodily resurrection provide stumbling blocks for many. There are a variety of solutions and explanations for the difficulties inherent in such doctrines; liberal theologians go to great lengths to do away with them.

The truth is, some doctrines of the Bible cannot be received except by faith. God's right to deal with us on

---

[1]The material presented in this chapter is based largely on Angus and Green, *The Bible Handbook*, pp. 272–275. See also Robert Tuck, *A Handbook of Biblical Difficulties* (London: Elliott Stock, 1900).

His own terms is not open to debate; it is not for the vessel of clay to contend with the potter (see Rom. 9:20).

There are some doctrinal subjects that are hard to interpret for a variety of reasons. Among these are the sanctification of believers and the whole range of *eschatology*.[2]

With regard to the matter of *sanctification*, the interpreter should note that there is much confusion because of the definition of terms. Some use the expression "the baptism *of, with,* or *in* the Holy Spirit" as synonyms for "the *fullness* of the Spirit"; others make a distinction between the terms. Various interpreters may stake their doctrine on one of these statements without considering the others. The question of sanctification must deal with two important issues: first, whether there is really a secret, invisible work of the Spirit apart from any emotional experience; and second, whether the Spirit of God has worked effectively in the believer to cleanse and control his life.

In addition, human experience varies a great deal from one person to another, depending on a number of factors. Therefore, personal experience ought never to be made the criterion for Christian doctrine. The declarations of Scripture should be the norm even though the *experiences* of people in the Bible also could be normative wherever they are ratified or explained by biblical statements. The Book of Acts is often taken as a norm for Christian experience. But we should note that its "pentecostal" experiences are to be understood in the light of doctrines set forth in the Epistles; because it is there that the Christian life is ex-

[2]Eschatology is the study of "last things," specifically, of prophecy that deals with the time immediately connected with the return of Christ.

pounded. The Book of Acts is primarily a history with a minimum of commentary.

Various doctrinal systems are not founded on the Scriptures as a whole or on a right interpretation. The church has always found it necessary to systematize its teaching; but the resulting systems are valid only when they are built on proper exegesis of the passages they treat and on the historical ordering of those texts.

Biblical *eschatology* may be classified generally in three divisions: (a) *post*millennialism, (b) *pre*millennialism, and (c) *a*millennialism. Postmillennialism teaches that Christ will return to the world only after the millennium. (Some postmillennialists believe this will be a literal 1,000-year period while others do not.) Premillennialism teaches that Christ will come again before the millennium; most premillennialists believe it will be a literal 1,000-year period. Amillennialism denies the reality of any earthly millennial reign, understanding it to represent the eternal state of righteousness and peace following Christ's return.

With regard to the three eschatological systems, the student should observe that the system resulting from any study of the subject depends on the interpretation given to the prophecies made concerning the nation of Israel and the prophecies concerning the church. Amillennialism contends that many of these prophecies are to be applied figuratively to the present gospel age. Premillennialism holds that such prophecies generally have a literal fulfillment. Postmillennialism interprets part of these prophecies literally and part figuratively. Keep in mind that the *sense* of Scripture is literal, even though it employs an abundance of figurative language. When the figures of speech may be resolved into substitute literal expressions, the sense is literal. On the other hand, literal expressions should not be turned into figurative ones. These principles should guide the interpreter in determining the validity of any eschatological system.

The premillennial system of interpretation predominates among most modern evangelicals. But among premillennialists there are three "schools" of thought with relation to the church in the period called "The Great Tribulation."

The *pre-tribulationists* hold that the coming of Christ is "imminent" in a special sense: that at His coming the church will be secretly raptured from the earth, before the Great Tribulation. They teach, too, that Christ will return (again) to earth after the seven years of tribulation and judgment. They believe that the church exists in a "parenthesis" in God's prophetic plan, and that it has no connection with Israel. Consequently, the larger part of the prophecies of the Book of Revelation and of Matthew 24 have to do with Israel and not with the church. This interpretation is part of *dispensational* theology.

Post tribulationists hold that Christ will not return twice, as the dispensationalists believe, and that His coming will occur only after the Great Tribulation. These interpreters belong to the *anti-dispensational* or *old premillennial* school. They hold that whenever a Jew is converted, he becomes part of the same people of God as the church (see Eph. 2:19-22; Heb. 11:39-40); that the church is the heir of the promises of God made to Israel and of its lot in the world; that the two groups will partake of the same kind of suffering in the Great Tribulation, without taking away anything from those prophecies spoken exclusively of the physical nation of Israel.

The *mid-tribulationists* teach that the church will suffer approximately half of the Tribulation and will then be taken up to be with Christ before the last judgments of that period. These interpreters seem not to worry about the relationship between Israel and the church, being interested more in the events of the Book of Revelation. They see the church raptured at one of several possible points during the Tribulation.

In determining which eschatological system to accept, the interpreter will find it necessary to examine the scriptural basis of each one, specifically: (1) the biblical statements that determine the relationship between Israel and the church; (2) the time of the rapture of the church; and (3) whether the rapture of the church is to be secret and invisible to the rest of the world.

Another kind of doctrinal difficulty is found in the apparent contradiction of certain biblical teachings. Galatians 6:2 and 6:5 seem to be in open conflict. Verse 2 says, "Bear one another's burdens"; but verse 5 says "For each one shall bear his own load." The Greek word (*barē*) translated as "burdens" means a moral burden, while the Greek (*fortion*) translated "load" means a responsibility. Verse 2 speaks of the attitude of love for Christian brothers who have problems, while verse 5 speaks of one's responsibility before God.

Proverbs 26:4 and 26:5 also appear to contradict each other. Verse 4 reads, "*Do not answer* a fool according to his folly/Lest you also be like him." Verse 5 reads, "*Answer* a fool according to his folly,/Lest he be wise in his own eyes." Each of the two texts limits the other, indicating under what circumstances it is proper to answer a fool according to his folly. Verse 4 teaches that one ought *not to talk like a fool*. Verse 5 recommends that a person *reprove* the fool, using words that he deserves; sometimes words like the fool's will help him understand his own foolishness.

In Luke 16:18 and Mark 10:11–12, divorce is prohibited in absolute terms. But in Matthew 5:32 and 19:9 it is allowed in cases of adultery or fornication. Then in 1 Corinthians 7:15 the husband is given the liberty of separating from the unbelieving wife *if she so chooses*. The absolute prohibition should be regarded as a general expression that has its exception: *the breaking of the marriage vow*. The two exceptions are in the same category: adultery violates the exclusiveness of the physical relationship, while desertion of one's mate is the denial of the promised care and fulfillment.

Sometimes a historical teaching or a biblical teaching is particularly difficult to accept because of moral issues involved. The case of Jephthah in Judges 11:24–40 would seem to sanction human sacrifice. Verse 31 tells of his vow to the LORD. "I will burn as an offering the first person that comes out of my house to meet me, when I come back from the victory. I will offer that person to you as a sacrifice." (GNB). Nevertheless, human sacrifices were expressly prohibited according to Deuteronomy 12:30–31; Leviticus 20:2; Psalm 106:37–38.

Jephthah may have dedicated his daughter to perpetual virginity, rather than to death (see v. 39). But if he *did* sacrifice her as a burnt offering, he did so because he misunderstood the will of God with regard to his duty. Furthermore, the age in which he lived was characterized by disregard for the law: "In those days there was no king in Israel; everyone did what was right in his own eyes" (Judg. 21:25).

A number of Psalms seem to show a vengeful spirit

rather than the Christian attitude of forgiveness. However, some of those expressions should be understood figuratively, as in Psalm 10:15: "Break the arm of the wicked." And again in Psalm 58:6: "Break their teeth in their mouth, O God! Break out the fangs of the young lions, O LORD." These petitions express the wish that God would take away the power of the wicked, and not that He would literally break their teeth or arms. The force of divine judgment on the wicked is emphasized in the figurative language of the Psalms.

Other expressions are prophecies of the sad end to come on those who rebel against God or the judgment of God Himself on those who disregard His law (see Deut. 28:15-68).

Note carefully that David was not lacking in the spirit of forgiveness, but prayed and fasted for his enemies in a true Christian spirit (see Psalm 35:12-15). His harsh expressions against his and God's enemies represent the divine attitude of condemning rebellion and the hardness of the human heart.

Certain acts of the prophets have been considered ridiculous or immoral. In some instances, they were symbolic acts, as in Isaiah 20:1-6, where Isaiah is told: " 'Go, and remove the sackcloth from your body, and take your sandals off your feet.' And he did so, walking naked and barefoot" (v. 2). Note that the word "naked" does not necessarily mean completely naked, but sometimes partially clothed, as in verse 4, "with their buttocks uncovered." Even so, the act was symbolic. Through Isaiah, God was revealing how the captives of Egypt and the exiles of Ethiopia would be led away in shame.

Other teachings or phrases have been interpreted without the necessary limitations.

Jesus' words in John 6:51–58 on the need of eating His flesh and drinking His blood are necessarily figurative and spiritual, according to verse 63: "It is the Spirit who gives life; the flesh profits nothing."

The rich man of Matthew 19:23, for whom it was "hard . . . to enter the kingdom of heaven" was one who *trusted in riches* for his entry into the kingdom" (Mark 10:24).

When we read in Matthew 5:30 that one should cut off his hand if it causes him to sin, it is to emphasize the great difference between the value of the body and the soul. Jesus was not really recommending such an act in a literal way; according to Mark 7:19–23, that would not solve the problem.

When we are told in Matthew 5:39 that we should "turn the other cheek" when we are slapped on one cheek, it is to put emphasis on the simple teaching in the first part of the verse: "I tell you not to resist an evil person," repaying one evil deed with another.

There are some teachings that are beyond our human comprehension, such as the eternal existence of the Godhead, the Trinity, the two natures of Jesus Christ in a single person, the absolute sovereignty of God versus the moral freedom of man, the value of prayer in conjunction with divine predestination or foreknowledge, and the problem of the origin of evil.

It should be remembered that the very nature of God implies virtues of infinite measure, making it impossible to search out many of His purposes and works. The presence of problems like those in the Bible is in complete harmony with the revealed character of God. If the Book that speaks on His behalf did not bear the imprint of anything that is beyond human comprehension, we would suspect it was merely a pious fraud. Thus, in one sense these doctrinal problems present additional evidence of the Bible's divine origin.

General Observations on Handling Doctrinal Difficulties:

1. The interpreter should first be sure that the difficulty is real, examining carefully any immediate conclusions.
2. All Scripture should be interpreted in agreement with what it claims to be: a completely inspired volume.
3. The Bible should be considered to contain a *system* of teaching from the beginning to end, and each book as a part of the whole.
4. At the same time, the earlier teaching of Scripture, particularly in the Old Testament, should be viewed as part of a progressive teaching, and subject to later revelation.
5. Obscure passages should always be understood in the light of what is clear, and not the reverse.
6. One should recognize the difference between doctrinal and historical difficulties; the former are resolved by faith, and the latter by means of thorough study, with the help of God's Spirit.
7. One ought not think that a satisfactory explanation will be found for every difficulty, given our present state of knowledge. Furthermore, the presence of elements that do not yield immediately to human reason in a book such as the Bible is a mark of its divine authorship.

Conclusion

At this point you will realize that the most important key to understanding the Bible is your own diligent study. Make it your goal to master the principles of interpretation, and to form the habit of applying them whenever you read. Underline important words and phrases and make notes in the margin with regard to proper interpretation.

Do not be discouraged about your ability to understand or to teach the Bible. While no one may claim infallibility in the study of hermeneutics, we do have an infallible Guide in God's Spirit. He promises to guide us into all His truth. God's Spirit must have the last word.

As Christian believers, committed to faithful handling of God's Word, we find ourselves under obligation to learn the rules of interpretation in order to carry out, as best we can, the ministry to which God has appointed us. The key to biblical interpretation is the interpreter's diligence in the pursuit of excellence: not for self-glory, but for the Lord.

"Be diligent to present yourself approved to God, a worker who does not need to be ashamed, rightly dividing the word of truth" (2 Tim. 2:15).

SUGGESTED BOOKS FOR
BIBLE STUDENTS

Bibles

The list below includes nine of the most widely used versions of the Scriptures. Reading more than one version is a great aid to the Bible student. Many Bibles are printed with additional study helps, which include alternate headings, introductions, and outlines of the Bible books, cross-references, and interpretative notes. Study Bibles and topical Bibles are not listed here.

Good News Bible (also called *Today's English Version*)

King James Version

The Living Bible (actually a paraphrase)

New American Standard Version

New English Bible

New International Version

New King James Version

New Testament in Modern English, translated by J. B. Phillips

Revised Standard Version

Commentaries

Books that help us understand the meaning and significance of the biblical text come in many varieties. They may be designed for the lay Bible student, the preacher, or the scholar. They may cover a portion of one book in the Bible, a complete book, or the whole

Bible. They may come in one volume or many volumes. They may take a devotional approach or be more concerned with scholarly exposition. They usually are based on only one version of the Scripture, sometimes the commentator's own translation.

Regardless of the kind of commentary being considered, the reader should be aware that all such books express certain doctrinal viewpoints as they comment on the biblical text. Consulting a commentary should be the last step in careful interpretation.

The few commentaries listed here are a small sample of the hundreds available and do not cover specific Bible books or smaller texts. They represent an evangelical approach to Scripture.

Calvin, John. *Calvin's New Testament Commentaries,* Torrance ed. (Eerdmans, 1979). The trustworthy, reformed classic, which set the standard for all later commentaries, is abridged and more accessible for the modern reader in this edition.

Guthrie, Donald, ed. *The New Bible Commentary,* rev. ed. (Eerdmans, 1970). A one-volume work with helpful commentaries on each book and interesting articles on Bible research.

Harrison, R. K. and F. F. Bruce, eds. *New International Commentaries* (Eerdmans, 1960–). A massive series (25 vols. projected on the Old Testament and 18 on the New) which contains both scholarly articles and readable introductions and commentaries.

Henry, Matthew and Thomas Scott. *Commentary on the Holy Bible,* 3 vols. (Nelson, 1979). This edition combines the popular, eighteenth-century commentaries of Henry and Scott and is based on the King James Version.

Tasker, R.V.G. *Tyndale New Testament Commentaries*, 20 vols. (Eerdmans, 1957–1971). See note under Wiseman.

Wiseman, Donald J. ed. *Tyndale Old Testament Commentaries*, 15 vols. (InterVarsity, 1979). Although published by different companies, both these series are popular with laymen due to their compact format and brief but perceptive comments.

Concordances

Concordances trace the words or topics in the Bible to the texts where they occur and are one of the most important reference tools for the Bible student. The concordances included in many editions of Bibles are usually not very complete. In Chapter 5 I mentioned *Strong's Exhaustive Concordance* and *Young's Analytical Concordance*, which some regard as superior to *Strong's*. Both these standards are available from several different publishers. A recent revised edition of *Young's* published by Thomas Nelson enables readers to use it with all contemporary translations as well as the King James Version.

Dictionaries and Encyclopedias

These reference books are indispensable for Bible study due to their detailed alphabetical listings of people, places, events, doctrinal themes, customs, and writings of the Bible. Maps and pictures are usually included. A Bible dictionary is limited to the words and terms in the Bible itself, while the encyclopedia covers anything deemed helpful in understanding the Bible and the ancient world. These two kinds of references supplement each other.

Davis, John D. *Davis Dictionary of the Bible* (Baker, 1979). Although this popular, conservative dictionary was first printed in 1924, its basic information is still sound.

Douglas, J. D., ed. *The Illustrated Bible Dictionary*, 3 vols. (Tyndale, 1980) With a clearly written and up-to-date text and colorful illustrations, this set is also being issued in a one-volume edition with fewer illustrations.

Gehman, Henry S., ed. *The New Westminster Dictionary of the Bible* (Westminster, 1970). Pertinent information, black/white illustrations and color maps add to the value of this new edition of *The Westminster Dictionary of the Bible*.

Unger, Merrill F. *Unger's Bible Dictionary* (Moody, 1966). This highly regarded volume provides detailed discussions of doctrinal concepts and current information on Bible sites from a conservative viewpoint.

Bromiley, Geoffrey, ed. *International Standard Bible Encyclopedia*, rev. ed., 4 vols. projected (Eerdmans, 1979–). Originally edited by James Orr and long recognized as comprehensive and reliable, the five-volume set is being revised to reflect new archaeological finds and current language study.

Handbooks

The handbook differs from encyclopedia and dictionaries because it lists articles in chronological order or according to the order of the books of the Bible.

Handbooks are usually less thorough than encyclopedias and give brief coverage to biblical research, but they are often more readable.

Halley, Henry, *Halley's Bible Handbook*, rev. ed. (Zondervan, 1976). The first book of this kind published and probably still the most popular, Halley's presents a conservative view of the background and authorship of Bible books.

Packer, J. I., Merrill C. Tenney, and William White, Jr., eds. *Bible Almanac* (Thomas Nelson, 1980). Well-illustrated and indexed, this helpful reference discusses a broad range of Bible topics in a popular style.

Harmonies

Especially useful in comparing the texts and teachings of various portions of Scripture, the best-known harmonies treat the synoptic Gospels.

Robertson, A. T. *A Harmony of the Gospels* (Harper, 1932). This standard reference contains extensive notes on special points of difficulty as it traces all the Gospel accounts of Jesus' life.

Throckmorton, Burton H., Jr. *Gospel Parallels*, rev. ed. (Thomas Nelson, 1979). Using the Revised Standard Version text, this harmony provides more critical help for the serious Bible student.

Hebrew and Greek Reference Works

In choosing a study aid for the languages of the Bible, the main consideration is to what extent the student already knows biblical Hebrew and Greek.

The list here includes books for both students who have some language background and for those who don't.

Archer, Gleason, A. Laird Harris, and Bruce Waltke. *Theological Wordbook of the Old Testament,* 2 vols. (Moody, 1980). Providing both theological importance and etymology, this is certainly the most complete reference for Old Testament word study. Because of its arrangement, the lay student may need to consult Strong's Concordance to locate a Hebrew term.

Bauer, Walter. *A Greek-English Lexicon of the New Testament,* ed. by William F. Arndt and F. Wilbur Gingrich (Univ. of Chicago Press, 1979). All serious students of New Testament Greek rely on this standard, which has been updated to include recent advances in linguistics.

Brown, Francis, S. R. Driver, and Charles A. Briggs. *A Hebrew and English Lexicon of the Old Testament,* rev. ed. (Clarendon, 1972). Some knowledge of Hebrew is required to use this reference, but its excellence has made it a standard of Old Testament study.

Robertson, A. T. *Word pictures in the New Testament,* 6 vols. (Broadman, 1943). This old favorite reveals word meanings that do not customarily come through in the word-for-word translation.

Trench, Richard C. *Synonyms of the New Testament* (Eerdmans, 1950). With an elementary knowledge of Greek, the student finds very helpful comments in comparative studies of New Testament words.

Unger, Merrill F. and William White, Jr., eds. *Nelson's Expository Dictionary of the Old Testament* (Thomas Nelson, 1980). Especially helpful for the

Bible student who does not know Hebrew, this book treats the most common Hebrew terms in simple style.

Vine, W. E. *Expository Dictionary of New Testament Words* (Thomas Nelson, 1978). Considered by some as the best one-volume reference for studying New Testament Greek, it gives good definitions and synonyms.

Interpretation

Biblical interpretation, like any other field of study, has a history of development and certain recurring issues. The books listed here discuss these subjects as well as the types of biblical literature and principles of interpretation.

Mickelson, A. Berkeley. *Interpreting the Bible* (Eerdmans, 1963). An extensive and solid treatment, this is also somewhat technical.

Ramm, Bernard. *Protestant Biblical Interpretation*, 3rd ed. (Baker, 1970). Emphasizing the contributions to interpretation of the reformers, this classic text surveys various types of biblical literature in a style suitable for lay students.

Sterrett, T. Norton. *How to Understand Your Bible* (InterVarsity, 1974). A very practical volume designed for the student without an extensive biblical preparation.

Fee, Gordon D. and Douglas Stuart. *How to Read Your Bible for All It's Worth.* (Zondervan, 1982). With special emphasis on the setting, purpose, and message of individual Bible books, this readable book for laymen reflects the solid scholarship of its authors.

BIBLIOGRAPHY

Abbott-Smith, G., ed. *Manual Greek Lexicon of the New Testament*. Edinburgh: T & T Clark, 1950.

Aland, Kurt, Matthew Black, Bruce Metzger, and Allen Wikgren, eds. *The Greek New Testament*. New York: American Bible Society, 1966.

Angus, Joseph, and Samuel G. Green. *The Bible Handbook: An Introduction to the Study of Sacred Scripture*. London: Religious Tract Society, 1905.

Barry, George Ricker, comp. *Classic Greek-English, English-Greek Dictionary*. Chicago: Wilcox & Follett, 1927.

Bernard, Thomas Dehaney, *The Progress of Doctrine in the New Testament*. New York: American Tract Society, 1940.

Calvin, John. *A Commentary on a Harmony of the Evangelists, Matthew, Mark, and Luke*. Grand Rapids: Eerdmans, 1949.

Cowan, Marvin. W. *Mormon Claims Answered*. Salt Lake City: Distributed by Conservative Baptist Home Mission Society, Wheaton, Ill., 1975.

Deane, Anthony C. *The World Christ Knew*, 1st ed. East Lansing, Mich.: Michigan State College Press, 1953.

Dunbar, Howard H., Mildred E. Marcett, and Frank H. McCloskey. *A Complete Guide to Good Writing*. New York: Heath, 1951.

Gehman, Henry S., ed. *The New Westminster Dictionary of the Bible*. Philadelphia: Westminster, 1970.

Gore, Charles. *The Sermon on the Mount*. London: John Murray, 1900.

Graham, Billy, *The Holy Spirit*. New York: Warner, 1980.

Halley, Henry H. *Compendio Manual de la Biblia*, 19th ed. Translated by C. P. Denyer. Chicago: Moody Press, 1965.

International Standard Bible Encyclopedia, 5 vols., 1st ed., ed. James Orr. Grand Rapids: Eerdmans, 1939.

Liddell, H. G., and Robert Scott. *Greek-English Lexicon*, rev. ed. Edited by Henry S. Jones. Oxford: Oxford Univ. Press, 1940.

Lohse, Eduard. *The New Testament Environment*. Nashville: Abingdon, 1976.

Macchi, Luis S. *Nociones de Sagrada Hermenéutica; O Introducción a los Libros Sagrados del Antiguo Testamento*. Buenos Aires: Sociedad Editora Internacional, 1943.

McQuilkin, Robert C. *Studying Our Lord's Parables*, 2 vols. Columbia, S.C.: Columbia Bible College, 1938.

Mickelsen, A. Berkeley. *Interpreting the Bible*. Grand Rapids: Eerdmans, 1963.

Ramm, Bernard. *Protestant Biblical Interpretation*. Grand Rapids: Baker Book House, 1956.

_____. *A Handbook of Contemporary Theology*. Grand Rapids: Eerdmans, 1966.

Sagrada Biblia, La, Torres Amat version. Santiago, Chile: Revista Católica, 1946.

Sanday, W. *Inspiration: Eight Lectures on the Early History and Origin of the Doctrine of Inspiration*. London: Longmans, Green, 1896.

Saphir, Adolph. *The Divine Unity of Scripture*. London: Hodder and Stoughton, 1906.

Schaff, Philip. *History of the Christian Church*, vol. 2, 5th ed. Grand Rapids: Eerdmans, 1910.

Sterrett, T. Norton. *How to Understand Your Bible.* Downers Grove, Ill.: Inter-Varsity, 1974.

Summers, Ray. *Worthy Is the Lamb.* Nashville: Broadman, 1951.

Trench, Richard Chenevix. *Notes on the Parables of Our Lord.* New York: Appleton, 1854.

Tuck, Robert A. *A Handbook of Biblical Difficulties.* London: Elliot Stock, 1900.

Vernon M. Grounds Learning Center. Brochure published by the Learning Center. Denver, 1980.

Webster's Seventh New Collegiate Dictionary. Springfield, Mass.: G & C Merriam, 1961.

Westcott, Brooke Foss, *The Epistle to the Hebrews.* London: Macmillan, 1906.

Wight, Fred. H., *Manners and Customs of Bible Lands.* Chicago: Moody, 1952.

INDEX OF TEXTS MENTIONED

Genesis

1:5 113
1:1–2:3 205
1:27 202
1:28 55
2–3 32
2:4–25 205
2:7 197
2:7–23 202
2:17 32
2:21–23 37
2:24 55
3:3 165,167
3:14–19 177,185
3:15 185
3:20 50
3:22 112
4:1 101
4:17 58
5:4 58,67
6:7 41,115
6:9 49,50
6:12 96
6:13–18 184
6:15 205
7:3 41
13,19 64
13:10,16 93
15:1 95
15:5 93,98
15:6 87
17:13 113
18:12 52
18:11–13 52
19:3 73
19:5 101
22:18 193
23:16 73
24:16 50
25:1–2 52
29:23 73
29:31–34 109
30:3 68
31:7 130
31:14–16 69
31:19 68
31:42 96
37:1 205
38:9–10 41
39:7 101
39:20 204
40:9–41:32 131

42:17–18 114
44:29 50
45:7 124
49:4 101
49:9 153
50:19–21 124

Exodus

2:11–15 64
3:15 112
4:12 97
4:16 173
7:1 173
8:19 114
12:14 112
12:40 203
19:5 . . . . .83, 87
21:6 195
33:11 . . . . .114, 205

Leviticus

2:11–12 127
18:5 83
18:6–20 101
19:18 142
20:2 211
25:45–46 113

Numbers

12:8 159
13:32–33 98
21:4–9 121
21:27 164
23:19 115
25:13 113

Deuteronomy

1:28 98
5:2–3 110
6:5 142
6:25 83
12:30–31 211
18:15–18 120,187
18:18 119
18:20–22 184
23:13 100
23:25 71
27:11–14 69
27:26 83
28:2 83
28:15–68 212
29:4 197

33:27 112

Joshua

1:15 120

Judges

7:12 93
9:7 69
9:7–20 157
11:24–40 211
14:14 158
21:25 211

Ruth

1:20 50

1 Samuel

9:9 174
10:11–12 162
21:1 203
24:13 162
28:16–19 184

2 Samuel

7:10–16 120,187
7:13 113
18:33 98

1 Kings

11:1–13 66
12:5, 12 113
18:27 98,101

2 Kings

4:29 72
14:9–12 157
18:27 23

2 Chronicles

18:26 126

Nehemiah

8:1–8 12

Esther

1:8 50

Job

3:16–19 170
3:21 70
6:5 166
9:2 83

12:2 97
25:4 83
38:31 98

Psalms

1:1 170
9 171
10 171
10:15 212
14:1 52
16:9–10 97,182
18:11 115
19:2 166
19:7–8 50
19:7–9 172
22 187
23 155
24:2 166
25 171
27:1 169
32:1,2,8 84
34 171
35:12–15 212
35:15–16 170
35:26 169
40:6 194
51:5 55,56
58:6 212
72 177
78:2–3 190
84:11 95
93:3 166
97:7 194
105:18 204
106:37–38 211
110:4 120
111 171
112 171
119 171
124:7 127
127:1 167
145 171

Proverbs

1:1–6 169
1:20–23; 24–33 100
2:4 70
2:21 166
4:25–26 172
5:15–18 96
5:18–19 101
6:2 166
6:16–19 170
6:30–31 98
8:1–31 100
8:10 . . . . .108, 172
9:1–6 155
14:1 167

14:34 167
15:29 167
16:22 95
17:22 167
20:20 131
21:30 172
23:1–2 98
23:23 96
23:29–30 172
25:4–5 94
25:18 95
26:1 93
26:3 93
26:4–5 210
26:18–19 93
30:15–16 171
30:18–31 172

Ecclesiastes

1:2–11 53
1:9 52
3:1–8 172
6:6 57
7:1 103
9:5 54

Song of Solomon

1:3 102
2:3–5 94
2:12 127
4:16 99

Isaiah

1:3 . . . . .99, 167
1:6 127
1:8 93
3:15 95
5:1–7 154
7:13–17 187
9:14–15 95
11:1 196
11:3–4 120
11:10 . . . . .192, 194
14:8 100
20:1–6 212
29:10 197
31:5 127
32:12 97
32:14–15 113
35:1–2 100
37:3 162
40:3 191
40:7–8 95
40:22 78
40:31 . . . . .127, 170
44:23 100
52:9 99
52:13–53:12 187

53 . . . . .33, 78
54:8 167
55:3 120
55:6–7 169
55:12 99
55:12–13 186
60:1 196
60:15 112
60:17 172
61:1–2 . . . . .120, 179
61:3 127
64:4 197

Jeremiah

7:13 115
23:5–6 120
25:11 184
48:10 172

Ezekiel

16:1–43 155
16:44 162
17:3, 22, 23 131
23:3 23
26:3–5 180
26:7 180

Daniel

5:25–28 184
5:30–31 184
6 31
7:2–8 65
7:4 126
9:2 184
12:4 78
12:9 79

Hosea

2:23 197
6:6 . . . . .110, 172
11:1 178

Joel

2:24 127
2:31 96

Jonah

2:5–6 127

Micah

4:3 97

Zechariah

9:9 120
13:7 182

Malachi

3:1 191

Matthew

1:5 204
1:1–16 . . . . .76, 199
2:1–12 38
2:15 178
2:22–23 200
2:23 195
4:3–11 202
4:18–22 199
5–7 201
5:4, 5, 6 102
5:10, 12 102
5:13 . . . . .146 151
5:14 . . . . . . .95, 146, 151
5:15–16 . . . . . . .145, 149
5:17–20 84
5:18 . . . . .50, 175
5:20 . . . . .81, 110
5:25–26 149
5:29–30 . . . .98, 149, 213
5:32 211
5:39 213
5:45 111
6:2–4 149
6:9–15 200
6:19–21 149
6:22–23 149
6:24 . . . . .145, 149
6:26 149
7:2 146
7:3–5 151
7:9–11 149
7:12 50
7:17–20 149
7:24–27 . . . . . . .147, 149
8:20 149
8:21 72
8:22 . . . . .146, 149
8:28–34 200
9:2–8 60
9:12 151
9:13 110
9:15 . . . . .145, 149
9:16 151
9:17 151
9:18, 23–36 60
9:37–38 149
10:9–10 201
10:24–25 149
10:31 111
11:16–19 150
12:1 71
12:11–12 150
12:25–26 149
12:28–29 149
12:40 . . . . .114, 120

12:42 120
12:43–45 150
13:2 137
13:1–9 . . . .137, 138, 147
13:4, 19 . . . . . .127, 141
13:10–17 133
13:18–23 . . . . . .137, 139
13:24–30 . .139, 140, 147
13:31–32 147
13:33 . . . . .127, 147
13:35 191
13:37–43 140
13:44 . . . . .70, 147
13:45–46 147
13:47–50 147
13:52 150
13:57 151
14:12, 19, 23 162
14:15–21 27
14:22–33 28
15:13 151
15:14 . . . . .21, 150
15:26 . . . . .151, 160
16:6 151
16:17–19 . . . . . . .33, 205
17:25–26 150
18:12–14 147
18:21–35 147
19:9 211
19:23 213
19:23–26 110
20:1–16 147
21:1–11 120
21:28–32 147
21:33–44 . . . . . .136, 147
22:1–14 . . . . . . .136, 147
23:25–26 150
23:37–38 99
24 209
24:17 51
24:26–33 58
24:32 . . . . .58, 65
24:32–33 . . .58, 147, 149
24:42–44 . . . . . .147, 150
24:45–51 147
25:1–13 147
25:14–30 147
25:32–33 150
26:23–25 184
26:31 . . . . .182, 184
26:34 . . . . . .63, 184, 205
26:48–49 184
26:56 184
26:69–75 . . . . . . .63, 184
27:24 126
27:37 61
27:63–64 114

Mark

1:2–3 191
1:15 . . . . .43, 121
2:2–12 60
2:17 151
2:19–20 149
2:21 151
2:22 151
2:26 203
3:23–26 149
3:27 149
4:2–9 147
4:13 137
4:21–22 149
4:24–25 149
4:26–29 147
4:30–32 147
4:39 99
5:1–20 200
5:23 60
6:4 151
6:8–9 201
7:4 47
7:19 101
7:19–23 213
7:27 151
8:15 151
8:31 114
9:43–44 149
9:44 113
9:50 151
10:11–12 211
10:24 213
10:45 79
13:28–29 149
13:33–37 148
14:30 . . . . .63, 205
14:61–62 102
14:66–72 63
15:26 61
16:16 58

Luke

1:3–4 76
2:1 97
2:39 200
3:14 46
3:23–38 199
4:1–13 202
4:18–19 . . . . . . .120, 179
4:23 . . . . .151, 162
4:24 151
5:1–11 200
5:17–26 60
5:31–32 151
5:34–35 149
5:36 151

228

5:37–39 151
6:12–16 201
6:17–49 201
6:38 149
6:39 150
6:40 149
6:41–42 151
6:43–45 149
6:47–49 149
7:11–17 72
7:31–35 . . . . . .111, 150
7:40–43 148
8:4–15 147
8:16–17 149
8:26–39 200
8:41, 42, 49 60
9:3 201
9:58 149
9:60 149
9:62 151
10:2 149
10:4 71
10:6 111
10:11–12 162
10:25–29 142
10:25–37 148
10:30–37 142
10:39–40 . . . . .24, 150
11:2–4 200
11:5–8 148
11:11–13 149
11:17–18 149
11:21–22 149
11:24–26 150
11:34–36 149
11:39–40 150
12:1 151
12:16–21 148
12:18–19 147
12:24 149
12:33–34 149
12:35–40 . . . . .147, 150
12:42–48 136
12:58–59 149
13:6–9 148
13:20–21 147
13:24–30 150
14:5–6 150
14:12 108
14:14 109
14:15–24 148
14:26 109
14:28–30 150
14:31–32 150
14:34–35 151
15:1–2 143
15:1–7 . . . . . . .147, 148

15:7 58
15:8–10 148
15:11–32 . .143, 144, 148
16:1–13 148
16:9 58
16:13 149
16:18 211
16:19–31 148
17:7–10 148
18:1–8 148
18:9–14 148
18:14 110
19:11–27 148
21:29 65
21:29–31 . . . . . .65, 149
22:36 . . . . .151, 159
23:34 123
23:38 61
23:43 123
24:46 114

John

1:14 77
1:18 205
1:21, 45 119
1:29, 36 . . . . . .83, 127
1:35–42 200
1:49 120
2 126
2:19 114
3:8 150
3:14–15 . . . . . .121, 122
3:15 121
3:15–16 122
3:29 151
4:19, 44 120
4:35–38 151
5:39–40 23
6:51–58 213
6:63 213
7:38–39 126
8:31–32 41
8:35 151
9:4 151
10:7 95
11:1–45 72
11:9–10 151
12:24–25 . . .93, 110, 151
12:25 110
13:10 151
13:10–11 190
13:16 151
13:38 63
14:12, 19, 23 162
15:1 95
15:1–8 155
15:20 151

16:21 151
16:23,25 79
16:25–29 159
18:16–17,25–27 63
19:19 62
21:15 . . . . .111, 127
21:18–19 160

Acts

1:25 101
2:25–32 120
2:25–31 97,182
2:40 57
3:22–26 120
3:25 111
7:23–35 64
7:37 119
10:40 114
17:11 16
17:28 196
18:6 115
20:35 . . . . .196, 204
21:11 184
21:33 184
26:7 83
27:22–26 184
27:34 98
27:44 184

Romans

2:12 50
3:21–22 56
3:23 121
4:6–8 84
5:10,12,15,17 . . .40,121
5:14 119
6:23 45
7:2 50
7:23 50
8:3 114
8:9 21
8:26 45
9:20 207
9:25 197
9:31–33 83
11:8 197
15:4 23
15:12 193,194

1 Corinthians

1:14–17 58
2:6–8 58
2:8 53
2:9 53,58,197
2:10 53
2:12 21
3:2 116

229

3:10–15 154
3:11 205
5:7 127
7:15 211
11:27 39,97
11:29 40
13 46
15:4 114
15:19 38
15:45 197
15:55 99

2 Corinthians

1:24 17
5:5 38
5:21 121
12:11 98

Galatians

1:11–12 22
2:2 22
2:3–21 84
3:5 116
3:11 50
3:16 193
3:17 203
4:22–31 154
4:24–31 32
5:11–12 104
5:23 50
6:2,5 210

Ephesians

1:3–10,15–23 40
1:7 124
2:3 111
2:19–22 209
5:6 111
5:8 111
5:14 196
5:21–22,25–33 58
5:26 126
6:14 44

Philippians

3:2–3 103
4:13 41

Colossians

1:15–19 61
2:20–23 58

1 Thessalonians

2 25
4:15 46
5:27 17

1 Timothy

4:16 57
6:10 38
6:16 115

2 Timothy

2:15 25,136,215
3:15–17 17
4:1 120

Titus

1:12 196
2:11–15 124

Philemon

11 103

Hebrews

1:1–3 61
1:6 194
1:9 127
4:2 24
4:8 120
5:1–10 120
6:20–7:25 120
7:12 53
7:13–18 53
7:25 121
8:1–2 53
8:6–13 53
8:7,13 85
9:23 111

10:5 194
11:17–19 119
11:39–40 209
13:4 55
13:10,15 53

James

1:25 50
1:27 97
2:23 56
2:24 56
2:25 56
2:26 56
3:5–6 150
5:14 127
5:20 57

1 Peter

1:12 177
3:3–4 110
5:8 126

2 Peter

1:9 21
1:19 176
1:20–21 18
2:7–8 64

1 John

1:7 96
2:20 127

Jude

9,14 196

Revelation

1:4–8 61
1:18 113
5:5 126
6:1–11 177
6:6 127
6:16 99
13:1–2 65
18:2 127
19:10 187
22:1 127